# CLONING

CLO

# NING

## Daniel Cohen

TWENTY-FIRST CENTURY BOOKS
BROOKFIELD, CONNECTICUT

Illustration credits: *Brave New World* (jacket cover) used by permission of
Bantam Books, a division of Bantam Doubleday Dell Publishing Group,
Inc.: p. 16; AP/Wide World Photos: pp. 29, 48, 99, 113; © 1997 Time, Inc.
Reprinted by permission: p. 37; Walter Iooss, Jr./Sports Illustrated/©
Time, Inc.: p. 43; Rothco Cartoons: p. 53 (top Tom Gibb, Altoona Mirror,
PA; center Shailo, © The Telegraph plc London; bottom Boileau,
Frankfort State Journal, KY); Photofest: pp. 65, 75 (TM & © 1992
Universal City Studios & Amblin); Photo Researchers, Inc.: pp. 81
(© Steve Maslowski), 90 (© Kenneth Edward/BioGrafx-Science Source);
Vince Warren/Oregon Regional Primate Research Center: p. 108; © Reuters
NewMedia Inc./Corbis: p. 123; © University of Wisconsin-Madison: p. 133

Library of Congress Cataloging-in-Publication Data
Cohen, Daniel, 1936–
Cloning / Daniel Cohen.
p. cm.
Includes bibliographical references and index.
Summary: Examines the history, current developments, future, and ethical
ramifications of cloning, recombinant DNA, and gene therapy.
ISBN 0-7613-2802-5 (lib. bdg.)
1. Cloning—Juvenile literature. [1. Cloning. 2. Genetic engineering.]
QH442.2.C64 1998 98-7015 CIP AC
571.8'9—dc21

Published by Twenty-First Century Books
A Division of The Millbrook Press
2 Old New Milford Road
Brookfield, CT 06804

# CONTENTS

# CLONING

## CHAPTER 1

# SOME HISTORY AND A HOAX

Cloning!

The idea seems to possess as much explosive potential at the end of the century as the idea of the atomic bomb had in the middle of the century. The power unleashed by nuclear physicists seemed to threaten the existence of the human species; the power unleashed by biologists seems to threaten the very idea of what is human.

Cloning has set off a wide-ranging and deeply emotional debate among scientists and the public in general. It has once again raised all the old questions, "Has science gone too far?" "Is what we are doing immoral?" "Should something be done just because it is scientifically interesting and possible?" "Are we invading God's realm?" It's Dr. Frankenstein all over again. And this time it's for real.

In *The Washington Post* an alarmed observer described a recent development in cloning as "one drop in a towering wave that is about to crash over us. The achievement will prove enormously valuable if it galvanizes us into readying ourselves for this inundation of helpful, treacherous, value-shattering and lifesaving information."[1]

And yet cloning is neither as "unnatural" nor as new as all the current public excitement would lead one to believe.

One definition of "clone," as given in *The Concise Columbia Encyclopedia,* is, "a group of organisms descended from a single individual through asexual reproduction."

In plants, reproduction by this kind of cloning is quite common, common enough to sometimes be called vegetative reproduction. The water hyacinth, for example, does produce seeds, but reproduces mainly by sending out underwater stems, which grow into new plants.

This is natural cloning and it can be extremely efficient. Under the proper conditions a handful of water hyacinths can quickly clone hundreds of thousands of new plants. The plants can spread so quickly that they literally block the passage of boats and become a serious menace to navigation.

Cloning is less common in animals, and until 1934 was completely unknown in vertebrates (animals with backbones). Then a team of scientists from the University of Michigan found a population of fish in northern Mexico that was entirely female. This species, known as the Amazon molly, is related to the tropical molly that is familiar in many home aquariums. Since that discovery other species of fish, amphibians, and reptiles that reproduce asexually have been found. So cloning among animals in nature is not unknown; it is not even rare.

Artificial cloning is also far from unknown and certainly isn't new. The word "clone" itself is derived from a Greek word meaning "twig." It comes from the ancient practice of taking a twig or cutting from one plant and either grafting it on another or rooting it to produce a new plant or shrub. It is an ancient practice in horticulture that may have begun at least four thousand years ago and is still a basic technique in gardening today.

Some varieties of grapes that are now used in the making of wine are clones of grapes that first appeared two thousand years ago. Because of their desirable qualities they were carefully preserved over the centuries.

If you have ever been to a place where apple trees grow unattended and in a semiwild state you would know that the apples they produce come in a variety of sizes and shapes, usually lumpy and irregular. In nature no two apples look the same.

Go to the supermarket and look at a pile of apples, particularly expensive ones. They are all the same size, shape, and color. The apples didn't turn out this way merely because of the way the trees were fertilized or watered—the apples are clones. When you bite into one of those perfect-looking Delicious or Macintosh apples you're biting into a clone.

Does it bother you?

Should it bother you?

As long as artificial cloning was limited to grapes, apples, and ornamental shrubs it was not regarded as a moral or ethical issue. The broader possible implications of cloning were not even realized until the middle of the twentieth century, though science fiction writers had sometimes speculated on the more far-reaching possibilities of cloning.

Cloning from single cells in the laboratory began with carrots in the 1950s. Scientists at Cornell University took cells from a mature carrot plant and put them into a gelatinous nutrient solution called agar. Isolated cells were then removed from the mass and cultured in another nutrient solution containing plant hormones. Within a few weeks embryonic carrot plants formed in the liquid environment. The experiment was so simple that it was carried out in high school labs.

There were jokes about monster cloned carrots. But still there was little discussion of the ethical implications of cloning carrots in the laboratory.

Then came the frogs. Cloning frogs in the laboratory was a lot more complicated than cloning carrots, but the problems were more a matter of technique than basic scientific theory. You can't just put a frog cell into a nutrient solution and expect it to grow into a new frog.

The only medium in which a frog clone will grow is the cell of a frog egg. Frog eggs are abundant, easy to obtain, and relatively easy to work with in the laboratory. Frog eggs are huge compared with eggs from mammals. That is why frogs were the first multicellular animals used in cloning experiments back in the 1950s. Scientists used a delicate glass pipette to suck the nucleus from the cell of a frog embryo and insert it into a frog egg from which the nucleus had been removed. It was a tedious, time-consuming, and often unsuccessful procedure.

The process is also not as easy or as straightforward as it sounds. The theory explaining how a frog could be cloned had first been proposed in the 1930s, but finding the exact tools and techniques with which the cells could be successfully manipulated took many years. Nobel laureate Hans Spemann, who laid much of the theoretical basis for successful cloning, referred to the manipulation of nucleus and egg as "a fantastical experiment." Actually the techniques and tools for carrying out such an experiment developed far more quickly than he had imagined. Less than fifteen years from the time he first proposed his "fantastical experiment" it was successfully accomplished. But it was one of those cases in which the operation was a success but the patient died. In the early experiments the eggs failed to develop beyond a very early stage. The reasons for this were not always clear.

It was fully two more decades before the techniques had been perfected to the point where the frog eggs actually continued to develop and hatch. Even then the experiments were not a complete success. Only the cells from embryonic frogs could be used. The eggs developed into tadpoles but they all died before they reached the adult frog stage. Still this marked an enormous advance, and it seemed only a matter of time until not only frogs but other more complex animals were successfully cloned.

The ability to clone frogs was a subject of compelling interest to the scientific community. It wasn't a matter of producing more or better frogs—there are more efficient ways of doing that. Scientists felt the experiments could potentially answer some important questions about cell biology, and that, in turn, could help scientists understand such things as the aging process and the development of cancer—big questions that can ultimately touch every human life.

But this sort of very basic, step by slow step science is not the kind of story that really captures the headlines or the public imagination. We look for something more easily understood, more immediate, more sensational. We want a "breakthrough." Embryo frogs do not qualify as a "breakthrough."

The interesting question was, "What else can be cloned?" So the question arose—if you can clone a frog can you also clone a human being? Theoretically, cloning frogs opened the door to the possibility of cloning other species, up to and including the human species. The problem was not one of basic biology, but merely of technique though the technical problems could be daunting indeed.

In 1979 cell biologist Robert Gilmore McKinnell, who had been actively involved in the frog cloning experiments, wrote, "Frogs were cloned some time ago. What about human cloning? Probably not soon—if ever. Why the difference? The difference is related to the nature of biological research. There is no need to clone humans to answer the questions that are central to cloning research . . .

"Efforts to clone humans clearly are not in the mainstream of biological research. Human cloning attempts will be costly and difficult. Certainly no scientific questions will be answered." But then he went on to add, "However, human cloning presents a challenge, and some people respond to technical challenge just as others, like some mountain climbers, respond to physical challenge. Therefore, it should not be surprising that occasionally someone will attempt human cloning . . ."[2]

Writers of science fiction had been speculating about the possible effects of human cloning long before it had entered the realm of reasonable scientific discussion. Certainly the most famous early fictional treatment of the subject was in the writer Aldous Huxley's 1932 novel *Brave New World.* This extremely popular and influential novel presented a grim and unattractive vision of a future in which human beings with different physical and mental abilities were cloned in order to do types of work for which they had been preordained.

Huxley's vision of a world in which babies were made to order in a factory was primitive in light of today's knowledge, but chilling nonetheless: "The first of a batch of two hundred and fifty embryonic rocket-plane engineers was just passing the eleven hundred metre mark on Rack 3. A special mechanism kept their containers in constant rotation. 'To improve their sense of balance,' Mr. Foster explained. 'Doing repairs on the outside of a rocket in mid-air is a ticklish job. We slacken off the circulation when they're right way up, so that they're half-starved, and double the flow of surrogate when they're upside down. They learn to associate topsy-turvydom with well-being; in fact, they're only truly happy when they're standing on their heads.' "[3]

Once the subject of human cloning became a topic of serious discussion among scientists it also became

*Brave New World* had been continuously in print for twenty years before this 1953 edition was released. The cover art was new but the message was the same—the story of a natural man in an unnatural, bioengineered world. On the back cover runs the line "an open-eyed, unforgettable look at a tomorrow that is frighteningly possible."

an increasingly popular topic for science-fiction writers. Cloning was almost never shown as something that would be of benefit to our species in the future. It was something scary, dangerous, and immoral.

In the 1970s the best-selling novelist Ira Levin, who exploited popular fears of Satanism in his book *Rosemary's Baby,* did the same for cloning with *The Boys from Brazil.* It's a novel about a fugitive Nazi scientist, working secretly in a jungle laboratory in Brazil, who is able to produce clones of Adolph Hitler. The popular book was turned into an even more popular film in 1978 with an all-star cast. Gregory Peck played the evil scientist.

There was another event in 1978 that had an even more profound effect on the public perception of human cloning. It was the publication of a book called *In His Image: The Cloning of a Man.* Only this time the book was not supposed to be fiction.

The author of the book was David Rorvik, a science writer of some reputation, and the publisher was the very respectable and conservative company J. B. Lippincott of Philadelphia. Though the book project had been turned down by other publishers the Lippincott endorsement was enough to get it serious attention. Rorvik had previously written a book of nonfiction titled *Brave New Baby: Promise and Peril of the Biological Revolution.*

The story Rorvik told was certainly a thrilling and exotic one—worthy of science fiction. Rorvik, a former science editor at *Time* magazine, said that in 1973 he received a telephone call from a sixty-year-old West Coast millionaire whom he called "Max." The childless millionaire wanted to produce a clone of himself and was willing to spend millions to do it. He had read Rorvik's previous book and wanted the writer to find a scientist who would help him. "My decision to recruit the medical talent required to clone a human being came after a long period of soul-searching," the author said.

The whole operation was to be conducted under the strictest secrecy. None of the participants were to be named, nor were their true identities even to be hinted at.

Rorvik went on to describe how he found a willing and knowledgeable scientist whom he called "Darwin." A secret laboratory was set up in an unnamed tropical country, somewhere "beyond Hawaii." Here there were a large number of poor women who were ready to supply eggs and try to carry the embryo clone to term. The women were told that they were taking part in an experiment to help infertile women. A cell from "Max's" body had its nucleus transferred to an egg without a nucleus from a selected "mother." A young woman given the name "Sparrow" was then chosen to carry the clone to term. Rorvik said the procedure had been a complete success, and the boy was born in the United States, presumably in California, in December 1976. The millionaire "Max" got what he paid for, a son and heir, just like himself. Strictly speaking a clone of the type described in the book would really be a long-delayed twin and not really a "son," or "offspring," in the usual way such terms are used.

Rorvik reported, "I have seen the child since his birth. He is alive, healthy, and loved today." It was a bit like *The Boys from Brazil* without Hitler.

Rorvik's book was due to be published in June 1978 but news leaked out early and created a sensation. The story of the cloned millionaire dominated the front pages of tabloid newspapers like the *New York Post*. BOY BORN WITHOUT MOTHER: HE'S THE FIRST HUMAN CLONE, the *Post* proclaimed in half-inch-high type across the front page. Stories about "the cloning of a man" appeared in practically every newspaper in the country. The stories asked not only "Is it true?" but "Is it right?"

The reaction of the scientific community ranged from cautious skepticism to outright denunciation. While the image of some lone scientist producing great "breakthroughs" in a secret jungle laboratory is a popular one in fiction, modern science does not work that way. If someone like Rorvik's "Darwin" was working so far ahead of everyone else in the field others would have known about it, if not in detail then at least in general. There would have been hints that experiments in human cloning were being conducted. Like everyone else, scientists gossip. Most scientific advances are already well known in the community of specialists long before they are announced to the general public. In this case there was no talk at all.

In the 1970s frogs and other amphibians had been cloned in the laboratory, but no mammals had ever been cloned. That wasn't for lack of trying. Scientists all over the world had been attempting to clone mice and other laboratory mammals, but without success. "Darwin's" accomplishment would have represented a monumental leap. Would any scientist really want to keep quiet about such an accomplishment, no matter how controversial it might be? That seemed highly doubtful.

While Rorvik gave only a vague description of the cloning process that was supposed to have been used many experts concluded that what he was describing was theoretically impossible and that Rorvick really did not understand the nature of cloning research. One expert called him "a functional illiterate in ethics and medicine." And that was not the worst thing that was said about him. In short, all sorts of warning flags were raised right from the start.

But even the possibility of human cloning, no matter how remote, touched off a furious public debate that resulted in, among other things, congressional hearings.

At first Rorvik said that he would welcome a congressional inquiry. However, when he was asked to testify things always seemed to get in the way. At first he canceled an appearance because of "personal health problems." He turned down a second scheduled appearance because he said he was on a tour of Europe to promote his book. The hearings were held without him. They essentially became a forum for those critics who denounced the book as a complete hoax—which in fact it was.

In the end the criticism hurt, and despite all the publicity the book didn't sell nearly as well as had been expected.

There is nothing illegal about making up a story and then publishing it as nonfiction. It had been done before, and has been done since and will be done again in the future. But Rorvik's troubles were mounting. He had used the names of real scientists in his book and one of them, British researcher Dr. J. Derek Bromhall, sued the publisher, claiming that he had been defamed because he had been named as having developed the scientific basis for human cloning. This lent credence to the claim that cloning had actually occurred. Dr. Bromhall also said that Rorvik had no authorization to quote from the doctoral dissertation in which Bromhall explored the possibility of human cloning. The doctor wanted the court to declare that the human cloning story was a piece of fiction.

The case dragged on for several years. Rorvik kept insisting that he would supply conclusive evidence of the truth of his account. But he never did, he just kept raising one objection after another. At one point he indicated that the cloned boy had developed a "defect." Bromhall's lawyer snorted, "This lends itself nicely to another revelation, namely, a convenient death of the alleged cloned boy and destruction of the proof of [Rorvik's] claim."

After three years a judge ruled the book to be a "fraud and a hoax." He said that it had been "finally and conclusively established" that "the cloning described in the book never took place." In 1982 the case was settled out of court for an undisclosed sum.

In retrospect it seems amazing that this obvious fraud managed to get as much attention as it did. But human cloning is a topic that touches deep human emotions. It was another fifteen years before the subject of human cloning was again passionately and widely discussed in the popular media.

And this time the trigger for the new excitement was no hoax.

## CHAPTER 2

# HELLO DOLLY

In the nearly two decades that followed David Rorvik's hoax the subject of cloning was consigned to the back burner as far as the public at large was concerned. But the scientific community had not abandoned all attempts to clone higher animals. A large number of research facilities throughout the world were working on various techniques for mammalian cloning. Progress had been painfully slow. So many experiments had failed that some scientists began to believe that there was something special about amphibian eggs, and that the nuclear transfer technique would never work with mammals.

In 1981, after some advances in technology, two scientists published a paper that stunned the scientific world, for it indicated that mammals could be cloned from embryo cells.

The researchers, Dr. Karl Illmensee of the University of Geneva and Dr. Peter Hoppe of the Jackson Laboratory in Bar Harbor, Maine, said that they had been able to transplant the nuclei of mouse embryo cells into mouse eggs from which the nucleus had been removed and produce three live mouse clones. Pictures of the mice appeared on the cover of the prestigious journal *Cell*.

Virtually everyone in the scientific community assumed that the article was correct. However, in science the results of a single experiment can never be fully accepted until the experiment can be reproduced by other scientists in other laboratories. There is always the possibility of bias or error in the original experiment and more frequently than most scientists like to admit there is also the possibility of fraud.

Other scientists tried to repeat the mouse cloning experiment, without any success. Two years after the original results of the cloning experiments had been published, other researchers found that some of them had been faked. Dr. Illmensee had been regarded by the press as sort of a scientific "wunderkind." He had been able to perform delicate genetic experiments that had defeated more experienced scientists. He got the reputation of having "golden hands."

But during the cloning experiments his colleagues reported he behaved suspiciously. He was reluctant to let even his laboratory assistants see what he was doing. When others failed to repeat his experiments he said that they simply did not have his skill at the delicate manipulations necessary for the experiments.

Because of Dr. Illmensee's fine reputation other scientists were reluctant to believe that he was faking his results, and even if they had suspicions they were extremely reluctant to accuse him of doing anything amiss. But by 1983 a mountain of evidence against him had been accumulated and the scandal broke. There was no formal punishment for Dr. Illmensee, but he did leave the University of Geneva to take a job with an obscure laboratory. He has not talked publicly about the events. Dr. Hoppe, who had coauthored the original study, was also investigated. No evidence against him was found, but his scientific career was ruined.

Another victim of the scandal was cloning research. The most impressive evidence for mammalian cloning had been discredited. The disheartening conclusion was that cloning mammals by simple nuclear transfer was probably impossible. An entirely new theoretical breakthrough might be needed, and who knew when that would come—if ever. Many scientists became afraid to venture into a field that had suddenly become controversial and tainted and where any advance would be viewed with suspicion.

Dr. James M. Robl, a cloning researcher at the University of Massachusetts, recalled that time in an interview with *The New York Times*. "Man it was depressing," he said.

After the first reports of Illmensee's cloning of a mouse came through there was tremendous enthusiasm. "We all thought we would be cloning like crazy." Dr. Robl started trying to clone cows and pigs, but nothing worked.

"We had a famous scientist come through the lab," Dr. Robl recalled. "I showed him with all enthusiasm all the work I was doing. He looked at me with a very serious look on his face and said, 'Why are you doing this?' "[1]

By the mid-1980s the once vibrant field of research had virtually collapsed. Funds dried up. People who had spent years conducting experiments in the area went into other more lucrative and promising fields. But not everybody gave up. Progress was being made, though it was painfully slow.

So when the "breakthrough" came it was so dramatic that the general public seemed stunned; even the scientific community was more than mildly astonished. Yet in a very real sense what happened wasn't a breakthrough at all.

No startling new insights into molecular biology had been developed. No basic questions about genetics had been answered, or even asked. The development was purely technical and there had been a tremendous amount of work in laboratories all over the world that led to the discovery—but it was stunning nonetheless.

A major reason for the surprise was that the crucial work had not been done in the laboratories of the leading universities or research institutions engaged in the high-profile, high-technology world of molecular biology. It came from the wrong side of the scientific tracks, a modest Scottish laboratory that has been primarily concerned with the very practical, humble, and unromantic business of breeding better farm animals. The Roslin Institute looks, and smells, more like a farm than a laboratory.

The first adult mammal to be successfully cloned was not a laboratory mouse, it was a sheep named Dolly. A cloned sheep caught public attention in a way a cloned mouse never could. A sheep is large and attractive. A mouse is, well, a mouse. It's hard to imagine a picture of a white mouse on the cover of a leading newsmagazine.

The Roslin Institute in Scotland where the experiment had been successfully carried out was created by the British government during World War II. During the war Britain was blockaded by German submarines and could no longer import food from other countries. With the country literally facing starvation Britain had to rely more than ever on homegrown products. Roslin's predecessor, The Animal Breeding Research Organization, was assigned to use the new field of genetics to help find ways of producing more food.

Dr. A. John Clark, a molecular biologist at the institute, told *The New York Times,* "You can feel the pressure these days to cure AIDS and cancer. It's hard to imagine now, but in the 40's there was the same pressure to make food. The place was put here to make food."

The scientists turned out to be very good at their job and they helped to make British agriculture as efficient as any in the world. By the 1960s the Roslin Institute was looking around for new projects to work on. The researchers chose to remake the Institute as a center for molecular biology and biotechnology, but always with the very down-to-earth aim of making livestock healthier, more efficient, and better able to serve humanity.

Most molecular biologists focus on the fine details of molecular interactions within the genes. And they work with small laboratory animals, like mice. The goal of the Scottish scientists, on the other hand, was a less scientifically exalted one. They were looking for ways to breed better sheep—in this case genetically altered sheep whose milk would produce proteins that could be useful in making drugs. Cloning was one step in the process, not the end product. The work was supported by a biotechnology company that wants to sell the drugs extracted from sheep's milk.

The head of the Scottish research team that produced Dolly was embryologist Dr. Ian Wilmut. He is well known and well respected in his field, the practical workaday world of research in livestock breeding. He is a pioneer in using frozen embryos in cows. Normally, cows give birth to just five or ten calves during a lifetime. By taking embryos produced by cows that provide the best meat and milk, freezing them, then thawing them and transferring them to surrogate mothers, Dr. Wilmut enabled cattle breeders to dramatically increase the quality of their herds. His work was very practical, more like technology than the sort of research that would result in an accomplishment that would electrify the scientific community and generate a flood of interest and an anguished debate among nonscientists as well.

Dr. Wilmut was by no means that figure so popular in science fiction, an isolated genius working alone in a secret laboratory. He wasn't anything like Rorvik's "Darwin." Such scientists don't exist in the real world and they never really did. Yet Dr. Wilmut was virtually unknown among molecular biologists who were supposed to be on the cutting edge of this research. That is one of the reasons that Dolly came as such a surprise.

Dr. Lee Silver, a biology professor at Princeton University who does genetic studies with laboratory mice, said, "I don't know him." He added that people who work with livestock "don't come to our meetings."[2]

Like many other scientists, Ian Wilmut had been interested in the possibilities of cloning mammals for many years. But when the Illmensee story broke in the early 1980s and scientists concluded that the research had apparently hit a brick wall, many researchers were left with the feeling that the technique which had once seemed so promising, indeed almost inevitable, might really be impossible.

Almost every cell in the body of frogs, mice, sheep, and human beings begins as a single fertilized egg cell. In the nucleus of that single cell is the DNA with all the information needed for the entire organism to develop. The fertilized egg cell grows and divides. The new cells specialize, becoming blood cells or nerve cells or skin cells or any one of the myriad of other specialized cells that make up a living organism.

But each of these cells, however specialized they become, still contains all the DNA found in the original fertilized egg cell. Each cell therefore contains the complete genetic blueprint necessary to produce another organism. In theory at least, the DNA in any cell in the body could be used to produce a clone of the creature from which the DNA had come.

That was the theory. But in practice it didn't seem to work very well. While there had been limited laboratory success with embryonic cells (those that had not yet become specialized) there was no progress at all in using cells from adult animals that had already devel-

Dr. Ian Wilmut in his lab in Scotland. In the months following
the disclosure of the successful cloning Wilmut traveled
extensively to describe the procedure to colleagues.
At one conference, he remarked that the cloning
technology "could easily do more harm than good."

oped and differentiated, even though all the necessary DNA was there. To many researchers it began to appear as though the problems associated with using genetic material from adult animals to create a new animal with the same genes might be insurmountable.

You might think that the progress in using embryo cells for cloning would generate enough excitement to keep researchers motivated and keep the funding for such experiments coming. But creating clones from embryos, while it is extremely important scientifically, is not the sort of work that grabs the headlines. The researcher who is making clones from embryo cells is essentially creating more twins. If an adult cell is used to make a clone the researcher has essentially created a genetic copy—a twin, if you will—of a fully developed creature that already exists.

Think of it in terms of the Rorvik hoax. "Darwin" the scientist could not create a copy of "Max" the childless millionaire if all he could do was clone embryos. The reason is obvious. "Max" was not an embryo. It is the possibility of cloning not just the fictional "Max" but the real Albert Einstein or Michael Jordan that rivets the attention and captures the imagination, not slow, steady, and undramatic progress in embryonic cloning.

Two of the leading researchers in the field published a famous scientific paper concluding that cloning an adult animal was impossible. Those few scientists who continued in cloning research concentrated on the easier and more promising task of cloning cells from early embryos. This research was enjoying some limited success, but not enough to shake the new belief that it was impossible to produce clones from adult cells.

Dr. Wilmut became a leader in the field almost by default. Very few other scientists were interested in pursuing that line of research anymore. It looked like a dead end.

Yet some progress in this area was being made. In the mid-1980s, Dr. Steen Willadsen, a Danish embryologist working in England for a biotechnology firm based in Texas, had successfully cloned a sheep using embryo cells. It was the first cloning of a mammal and it attracted quite a bit of attention at the time. But Dr. Willadsen went further. He was able to successfully clone a sheep from the cell of an embryo that had begun to develop. However, he never conducted any further experiments in this area and never even published his results of these experiments.

Dr. Wilmut heard a rumor about Dr. Willadsen's work in 1986. "I thought it was true," he said. "—if it was true we could get these cells from farm animals." Then it might also be possible to push the research further, to make clones from mature embryos and eventually from adults. He then began planning for the experiments that ultimately led to Dolly. It took years of hard and tedious work.

The key question that Dr. Wilmut and his colleagues had to answer was why had no one ever been able to successfully use a mature cell in cloning. Most of those in the field had concluded that something happened to a mature cell that made it impossible for it to be used in cloning, that a specialized cell permanently lost its ability to produce anything but other specialized cells. No matter approach what researchers tried, a skin cell would only produce more skin cells. Dr. Carl Pinkert, a developmental biologist at the University of Alabama in Birmingham, told *The Washington Post*, "This whole idea of cells being terminally differentiated was the dogma of our time. We thought there were irreversible genetic modifications."[3]

Dr. Wilmut and his colleagues in Scotland did not subscribe to the dogma of the time. They didn't believe that a new theoretical breakthrough was necessary to use adult cells in cloning. They assumed that the problem was strictly a technical one. Just find the right key, the right formula, and the DNA locked in the genes of adult cells could be used successfully in the standard nuclear transfer technique of cloning research just as embryonic cells had been used.

Dr. Keith Campbell, a biologist at the Roslin Institute, thought the key might be found in the life cycle of the cell. All cells go through cycles in which they grow and divide, making a whole new set of chromosomes each time. Dr. Campbell thought that the egg might be at one stage of its life cycle while the adult cell was at another, which would make them temporarily incompatible.

Dr. Campbell suggested that it might be possible to overcome this problem by slowing down and nearly stopping cellular activity in the donor cell. The best way to force the cell into a sort of hibernating state was to deprive it of certain essential nutrients—in a sense, starve it to sleep. Actually the technique had already been used, by accident. In 1994 a staff member at a Wisconsin laboratory forgot to provide the proper nutrient serum to cells that were being used in an experiment. The result was that in 1994 four calves were cloned. But the donor cells had been from an early embryo and the Wisconsin researchers at first failed to appreciate the potential significance of their own work.

In 1995, Dr. Wilmut and his associates used embryo sheep cells that had been grown for a short time in the laboratory to produce identical twin sheep clones they named Megan and Morag. The experiment was written up in the journal *Nature*. David Solter, a scientist who had a decade earlier said that cloning mammals was impossible, wrote an accompanying editorial that ended, "Cloning mammals from adult cells will be considerably harder, but can no longer be considered impossible; it might be a good idea to start thinking how we are going to make use of such an option."

This experiment was very nearly as important as the experiment that cloned Dolly, but astonishingly almost no one paid any attention to it. Not only was the general public unaware of what had been done, the scientific community, the biologists and geneticists, also largely ignored the work. That is one of the reasons they were so very surprised when Dolly came along. The work that was being done in Scotland was not secret, they had just not been paying attention.

In the experiment that led to Dolly the researchers removed cells from the udder of a six-year-old sheep. The cells were then essentially starved for five days in a petri dish. That made most of the cell's genes turn off. In this resting state the cells resembled undifferentiated embryonic cells.

That was the first step. The second step was "reawakening" the cell. In the past this had been done by giving the cell a meal of the nutrients of which it had been deprived. The problem is that when a cell is switched back on in that way it essentially "remembers" the kind of cell that it was, and it is useless in cloning experiments.

The Scottish researchers, with their practical approach, tried to find a way around the problem. They modified the technique for reawakening the cells. The quiescent nucleus of the donor cell was placed inside a sheep egg from which the nucleus had been removed— the standard procedure.

But the "combination cell" was then awakened not only with a meal of nutrient broth but with a mild jolt of electricity. The cell then began dividing as though it were an embryo. A clone had been produced from the genetic material in an adult cell.

Apparently there is something in the egg's cytoplasm that makes the donor cell "forget" what it was, and behave as if it were the nucleus of an egg cell. Just exactly how and why this happens is unclear, and it will take a great deal of careful laboratory work to understand what happens.

But even though the researchers didn't fully understand why the process worked, they knew that it did work, though not all of the time.

Dolly was the only lamb to survive from 277 eggs that had been fused with adult cells. Of the original 277 only 29 survived more than a few days. These were transferred into the wombs of adult sheep but only one fetus, Dolly, survived to term. Why this particular cell continued to divide and develop into an embryo, when so many others did not, also remains unknown. Further experiments will almost certainly improve the success rate, particularly since researchers from all over the world will now be attempting to refine the technique. The birth of Dolly has brought about a dramatic and explosive rebirth of scientific interest in cloning.

The experiment that produced Dolly was begun in the last week of January 1996. That was when the donor cell and egg cell were fused. When the resulting embryo was approximately six days old it was implanted in the womb of a ewe.

The first real indication that this time the technique was going to work came on March 20, 1996, the 48th day of Dolly's surrogate mother's pregnancy. After that the ewe was scanned regularly with ultrasound to check on the development of the fetus. With a great sense of relief and growing excitement, the researchers found that the pregnancy was a normal and untroubled one.

Dolly was born on July 5, 1996, at 4 P.M. in a shed just down the road from the Roslin Institute. It was a normal birth, head and forelegs first. She weighed about 14 pounds (6.6 kilograms) and was a healthy lamb.

The name Dolly, by the way, was an in-house joke, chosen because the lamb had been cloned from the mammary glands of an adult sheep. She was named after the well-endowed country-and-western singer Dolly Parton.

Those who attended this epoch-making birth were a local veterinarian and a few members of the Institute staff. One of them called Dr. Wilmut, who was at work at the Institute. He doesn't even remember receiving the call, and wasn't particularly excited at the time. "I even asked my wife if she could recall me coming home doing cartwheels down the corridor, and she could not," Dr. Wilmut told *The New York Times*.

The birth of Dolly was not announced immediately. There were patents on the process that had to be applied for since the research was funded by a biotechnology company that hopes to make money from it. Dr. Wilmut and his associates do not stand to make much money from their discovery.

"I give everything away," Dr. Wilmut said. "I want to understand things."[4]

While Dolly's birth was supposed to be a secret, like most scientific discoveries, it was a very loosely kept secret. Laboratory assistants and graduate students always exchange gossip. Rumors of the successful birth of a cloned lamb circulated for months through the corridors of scientific meetings. But the general public heard nothing until March 1997, when a paper describing the work was published in *Nature*. Unlike the paper that announced the birth of Megan and Morag this one was not overlooked. For the nonspecialist the article did not make exciting reading. Other scientists described it as "pure technology" or a technical manual for how to clone a sheep.

No matter how often Dr. Wilmut tried to stress the practical and technical aspects of his work the broader implications of success with Dolly could not be ignored. So the subject moved rapidly to the front pages of respected publications like *The New York Times* and the

Dolly on the cover of *Time* magazine from March 1997,
when her story first hit the major media.

covers of newsmagazines like *Time* and *Newsweek*, to the evening TV news, to jokes for Jay Leno and David Letterman, to an almost instant made-for-TV movie. Within days everyone was talking seriously about Dolly and the highly emotional subject of the possibility of human cloning.

Suddenly much to his surprise, and sometimes to his distress, the normally retiring Dr. Wilmut found himself famous—and, in the eyes of some, infamous.

CHAPTER 3

# CHAPTER 3
# THE CONTROVERSY

If scientists can clone a sheep can they also clone a human being? The answer to that question almost certainly is yes.

Of course, a human being is not a sheep but our reproductive processes are virtually identical. While there may be some unforeseen obstacles virtually everyone who is knowledgeable in the field now believes that human cloning is possible—and could be accomplished soon.

Way back in 1971, Dr. James Watson, a winner of the Nobel Prize for his codiscovery of the structure of DNA and author of an extremely popular book *The Double Helix,* which described the discovery, wrote an article for *The Atlantic Monthly* titled "Moving Toward the Cloned Man." The famous scientist warned that this was "a matter far too important to be left solely in the hands of the scientific and medical communities."

The real questions now are would human cloning be desirable? Should it even be allowed?

There is no general agreement at all about those questions. In fact, despite Dr. Watson's warning, until the appearance of Dolly there had been relatively little serious discussion of the subject of the ethics of cloning for many years.

When Nancy Duff, a professor of theological ethics at Princeton Theological Seminary, was asked by *The Washington Post* to write a post-Dolly piece on human cloning in the paper's commentary and opinion section, Outlook, she confessed: "Six years ago I reacted to an essay on the ethics of cloning by asking why anyone would waste time pondering the moral implications of something that could never happen. So much for my gift of prophecy."[1]

When the media descended en masse upon the once obscure Dr. Ian Wilmut of the Roslin Institute of Scotland, reporters didn't want to talk about better livestock or the possibility of producing lifesaving drugs in sheep's milk—they wanted to talk about cloning human beings.

In countless interviews Dr. Wilmut has insisted that his work has nothing to do with the cloning of humans, and that he can't understand why anyone would want to do something like that. But he did admit that the technology to clone humans is within reach, though he would personally find any such attempt "offensive."

Some animal rights activists have objected to cloning sheep or mice or indeed using any animals in experiments. In fact, in 1991 animal rights activists in Britain burned down two buildings belonging to the Roslin Institute lab. It was the first time the general public became even dimly aware that Dr. Wilmut and his colleagues were conducting cloning experiments.

However, the ethics of cloning sheep or mice is something that is of concern only to a small percentage of the population. The real controversy is over human cloning.

First let us deal with a couple of widespread misconceptions about human cloning. One of our darkest fears about cloning is the *Brave New World* image of hordes of clones produced for specific purposes, usually menial labor or warfare. Such fears come largely out of the misconception that cloned humans or sheep are actually "grown" in the laboratory. We have all heard the phrase "test tube baby." But that's not the way it works.

The initial steps are taken in the lab. The DNA from one cell is inserted into an egg from which the nucleus has been removed. The two cells are then fused and are allowed to develop and divide for a few days. After that the action moves out of the laboratory because if the tiny embryo is to survive, grow, and develop into a sheep or a human, that development must take place in the womb. The tiny embryo must be implanted into the uterus of a female of the same species.

With sheep that's not a big problem. There are plenty of sheep, and they have nothing to say about whether to become part of a cloning experiment or not. To produce large numbers of human clones, given the high failure rate in cloning procedures, far larger numbers of women would have to agree to undergo the repeated and sometimes risky surgery necessary to obtain eggs. Remember it took 277 tries to produce Dolly.

Even more significantly vast numbers of human surrogate mothers would be required. The number of women who would be willing essentially to rent out their wombs in order to grow clones is never likely to be very large. And the expense of producing even a single human clone would be enormous. It is far easier, safer, cheaper, and more pleasurable to produce offspring the old-fashioned way. That is not going to change.

Perhaps some day procedures can be developed with which an embryo can be fully grown in a laboratory, that a true "test tube baby" can be produced. Right now the practical and technical problems that would have to be solved appear overwhelming. They would require a genuine quantum leap in the technology of reproduction. There are no such procedures today and they are not on the horizon, not even for sheep. The frightening image of mass production of laboratory-grown clones is now strictly science fiction, and will remain so for a very long time.

Many of the articles on cloning that appeared in the aftermath of Dolly were illustrated with multiple images of famous people who might be cloned. Michael Jordan and Albert Einstein seemed to win the contest of most likely to be cloned when and if the technology is ever applied to human beings.

Like the phrase "test tube baby" the multiple images are very misleading. While a Jordan clone or an Einstein clone would be genetically identical to the original, they would not appear suddenly as an exact

One of the many "cloning" images created to accompany articles
about Dolly and the future of cloning. A team of Michael Jordan
clones was the immediate dream of his fans.

duplicate of the NBA superstar or the scientific genius. Cloning is not xeroxing. The clones would begin just as the original Jordan and Einstein began—hairless, toothless, and requiring diapers. They would be infants. They would not automatically inherit all of the memories of their genetic progenitor any more than we inherited the memories of our parents. The Jordan clone and the Einstein clone would have to grow, develop, and experience life as individuals just as the originals did.

Thinking of clones as exact duplicates is not only misleading it's really kind of scary. The clone then seems something artificial—not really human. It's far more accurate to think of clones as identical twins of different ages.[2]

Identical twins, even though they are exactly the same age, look alike, and may have grown up in the same environment, are still not exact copies of one another. Though they are genetically identical they each experience life a bit differently. They develop into similar but still very distinct individuals.

David Lebedoff, an identical twin, tried to reassure readers of *St. Paul Magazine* that though he and his brother share the same DNA, they are not the same. They don't have the same fingerprints. "Though we are monozygotic twins, slight changes started occurring even in utero. Maybe it was the crowding. After delivery, of course, there were differences in environment. My brother, for instance, seems to worry less than I do; was his incubator slightly warmer?

"My brother can't understand why I don't agree with him that *The Godfather, Part II* is better than the original. (As the last born, he may be predisposed to sequels.) He's a whiz at bridge, which I don't even play. If sheep could talk, you wouldn't need this article. Somewhere in that Scottish fold the ewes are murmuring that Dolly's younger sister doesn't wait as patiently in the food line as Dolly herself. They know that the two are not the same."[3]

The chairman of a government commission that reported on cloning was Harold Shapiro, president of Princeton University. He was particularly interested in the subject because he is an identical twin. He believed that a lot of the public concern that arose after Dolly was not based on fact but a "gut reaction" based on "vague" reasoning. He insisted that he was surprised that both he and his twin brother became university presidents. What are the odds against that? Genetics does not determine the course of an individual's life, but it obviously plays a role.

Beyond the genes, just imagine how much different development would be for a clone. The clone of Jordan or Einstein would be conceived in an egg taken from a different woman, and nurtured in the womb of a different mother. The effects of this should not be underestimated. Richard Strohman, a molecular biologist at the University of California, has pointed out that a mother's egg is not "an empty bag into which we can put new genes. Every egg is unique." Just exactly how the environment of a particular egg impacts on the development of an embryo is not precisely known, but it is certain that it would influence the development somehow. Furthermore the mother's behavior during pregnancy—what she eats, and whether she drinks or smokes—can have a significant effect upon her baby. So even at birth there would be profound differences between clone and "parent," or "twin."

Then there is the environment in which the cloned child would be raised. He would be of an entirely different generation, raised in a different time, place, and situation. In a very real sense the clone would be born and grow up in a completely different world than the original. He wouldn't have had *those* parents, *that* teacher, or *that* experience which helped to shape his life and give it direction. The result would inevitably be not only a distinct individual, but a vastly different one. The Jordan or Einstein clone might eventually look a lot like the original Michael Jordan or Albert Einstein, but he would not be Michael Jordan or Albert Einstein.

Among those scientists who study human development there is an ongoing argument over how much of what we are is due to "nature" and how much is due to "nurture." That is, what aspects of our health and personalities are the result of our genetic inheritance and what aspects are the result of our environment and life experience. There is no scientific method of determining the relative importance of the different factors and this perennial argument will probably never be resolved. But we can definitely say that both are involved and we are each a lot more than the sum total of our genes. It would be the same for a human clone.

And yet from the moment news of the cloning of a sheep became known there was an almost worldwide shudder of revulsion as people confronted the idea of human cloning.

The Vatican immediately condemned human cloning as an affront to human dignity. Within days of the publication of the *Nature* article, the usually slow-moving European Parliament proposed a formal Europe-wide prohibition on all research into human cloning. Other countries as diverse as Argentina, China, and Japan called for a ban on any effort to clone a person. Some already had laws that prohibited research in that area.

The United States had no such prohibitions on the books. But polls showed that a large majority of the people of the United States shared the rest of the world's worries and repugnance toward the idea. American politicians held hearings in Congress and state legislatures. Senator Christopher Bond (a Republican from Missouri) immediately introduced a bill in Congress to ban the federal funding of human cloning or human cloning research. "I want to send a clear signal," the senator said, "that this is something we cannot and should not tolerate. This type of research on humans is morally reprehensible." The state of California quickly enacted a ban on human cloning.

President Bill Clinton apparently felt the same way for he imposed a ban on the use of any federal money for research into human cloning and asked researchers supported by private money to hold off voluntarily.

"Each human life is unique," the president said, "born of a miracle that reaches beyond laboratory science. I believe that we must respect this profound gift and resist the temptation to replicate ourselves."[4]

Clinton also asked the National Bioethics Advisory Commission—a group that hardly anyone had ever even

Protesters outside the State Office Building in New
York during hearings on the implications of cloning.

heard of before—to examine the legal and ethical issues of human cloning. He gave them ninety days to come up with a report.

Normally a report by a body as obscure as the Bioethics Advisory Commission would attract absolutely no attention in Washington, which is awash with obscure commissions that regularly issue voluminous reports that few pay much attention to. But right from the start the deliberations of the commission were the subject of intense interest and often protest. At the very first public meeting animal rights activists seized the platform. One dressed as a sheep shouted, "Animals are not test tubes with tails!"

When the final report was issued it was in a televised ceremony in the White House Rose Garden on June 9, 1997. The president himself was there. It was carefully orchestrated to be a very high-profile event—concrete proof that the U.S. government is really concerned about the issue.

The commission report concluded that if the procedures that had created Dolly were used to create a human child it would be "a premature experiment" and "morally unacceptable." The report called for legislation prohibiting anyone from making the attempt either in research or a clinical setting. There were many other objections to human cloning contained in the commission report and a call for "much more widespread and careful public deliberation before this technology may be used."

The president proposed a bill based on the commission's recommendations. At a press conference he said that the ban would keep someone from "violating our most cherished beliefs about the miracle of human life and the God-given individuality each person possesses."

The commission's report was immediately attacked by both sides of the cloning argument. Those who were opposed to human cloning, the large and vocal majority, said it didn't go far enough and called for a ban on all research in human cloning forever. From the other side came the argument that these proposals represented an unacceptable roadblock to scientific research, which might produce results that would be of enormous benefit to mankind.

In the end the president's bill couldn't find a congressional sponsor. Bills that would place greater restrictions on research in human cloning have been proposed but it is anybody's guess what form they will take when and if they are ever adopted.

In short the political situation in the United States is muddled.

The most determined and irreconcilable objections to human cloning are religious. And many of them are similar or identical to the arguments used in the continuing battle over abortion, reproductive technology such as in vitro fertilization, and some fetal research.

A key question is, at what point does life begin? There were 277 failures before Dolly was produced. Would the inevitable failed attempts at human cloning during experiments represent the loss of individual human lives? Some religions hold that they would and as with abortion, these religions would condemn all such research as immoral and unacceptable. This is not a position that will be compromised.

Not all failures in cloning research are total. Sometimes a clone can be born with grave deformities and defects, though this did not happen in the research that resulted in Dolly. In animal research the defective clone is simply destroyed. Would that be the fate of a defective but still living human clone? All of the emotional and deeply divisive arguments over such topics as abortion and euthanasia are being replayed in the arguments over cloning—but with a new twist.

Even if failure could be entirely eliminated many religious leaders would still oppose human cloning. The Rev. Richard A. McCormick, a professor of Christian ethics at the University of Notre Dame, said the obvious motives for cloning a human were "the very reasons you should not."

He was concerned that people would see cloning as a way to replicate themselves, to "replace" a dying child, or to create someone who could be a compatible organ donor. The vision of the organs of clones being "harvested" as spare parts for their ailing "parents" is truly nightmarish.[5]

Cloning would tempt people to try to create humans with certain physical or intellectual characteristics, Father McCormick said, elevating mere aspects of being human above the "beautiful whole that is the human person."

"Who decides what are the desirable traits, what are the acceptable traits?" he asked.

Dr. Ruth Westheimer, the well-known sex therapist, based her objections on history. "I came out of Nazi Germany," she said. "If you could make people who were only Aryan, blond and blue-eyed, someone like me—Jewish and 4 foot 7—would not be here."[6]

Writing in the Catholic publication *Commonweal,* John Garvey goes even further: "There are ethicists who have no problem with the idea of cloning itself, but who worry only about its potential for misuse," he writes. "This strikes me as being tone-deaf to mystery, to any sense of the sacred . . . Retaining this sense of wonder could lead a scientist to say, 'Yes, we can do this; it would be interesting, and wrong.' That something can be done obviously does not mean it should be; but without a restoration of the sense of the sacred, of mystery, we will probably not be able to begin to make that argument, or even to understand it ourselves."[7]

Conservative columnist George Will worried that cloning could break down the very fabric of society. "Connections with parents, siblings and ancestors are integral to being human, although not to being a sheep." And social critic Jeremy Rifkin thundered that cloning "throws every convention, every historical tradition, up for grabs."

One of the most furious attacks on cloning was launched by Leon R. Kass, a onetime biochemist who actually quit the field because he was so appalled by what he considered a cavalier approach by many of his colleagues to cloning. Kass became a philosopher, ethicist, and full-time opponent of cloning. When the news about Dolly was released he wrote a cover story for *The New Republic* in which he warned of the confusion of relationships produced by human cloning. Not only will a parent be one's "twin," Kass said, but "all other relationships will be confounded. What will father, grandfather, aunt, cousin, sister mean? Who will bear what ties and what burdens? What sort of social identity will

There is always somebody ready to make light of a serious subject, and sometimes the humor is more on target than the discussions. These are some of the many cartoons to appear in local and national newspapers when the cloning argument was at its height.

'Who designed this baby?'

someone have with one whole side 'fathers' or 'mothers'—necessarily excluded? It is no answer to say that our society, with its high incidence of divorce, remarriage, adoption, extramarital childbearing and the rest already confounds lineage and confuses kinship and responsibility for children (and everyone else), unless one also wants to argue that this is, for children, a preferable state of affairs."[8]

One of the most frequently heard arguments against cloning is that it would tend to turn children into products and destroy their sense of personal identity. Rather than being unique and genetically distinctive individuals they would be laboratory-created to fulfill someone else's image of a perfect, or at least desirable, child.

Playwright Wendy Wasserman quipped, "What would I say to my shrink? I hate my parents? When I am my own parent?"[9]

Critics of human cloning believe that inevitably a clone would be produced to fulfill someone else's ideal. Kass wrote, "When a couple now chooses to procreate, the partners are saying yes to the emergence of new life in its novelty, saying yes not only to having a child but also, tacitly, to having whatever child this child turns out to be. Each child has a genetic distinctiveness. While parents certainly feel a biological connection to their offspring, and try to guide them in their development, the child is clearly recognized as an independent individual."

Would it be the same for a clone? Kass and other critics of cloning think not. "The child is given a genotype that has already lived, with full expectation that this blueprint of a past life ought to be in control of the life to come." What would happen if the Michael Jordan clone decided he wanted to play baseball rather than basketball? The original Michael Jordan tried that without much success. Or what if the Albert Einstein clone tried to take up playing the violin full-time? The original Albert Einstein was at best only an enthusiastic amateur violin player.

"Cloning is inherently despotic," writes Kass, "for it seeks to make one's children (or someone else's children) after one's own image (or an image of one's choosing) and their future according to one's will. In some cases, the despotism may be mild and benevolent. In other cases, it will be mischievous and downright tyrannical. But despotism—the control of another through one's own will—it inevitably will be."[10]

Try for a moment to imagine that you are a clone of your father or mother or even of some distant and distinguished ancestor. Would you feel compelled to follow in the footsteps of the original? Or would you feel an overwhelming desire to live so as to avoid the mistakes that the original made in his or her life? Would you ever feel like a fully independent individual? On the other hand, supposing you were the clone of a person with an unusual talent, would your parents be able to resist encouraging you in that direction?

In an essay in the summer 1997 issue of *Free Inquiry,* Richard Dawkins wrote, "But don't you whisper to yourself a secret confession? Wouldn't you love to be cloned?" This desire he admitted would be the result of "pure curiosity." He explained, "I find it a personally riveting thought that I could watch a small copy of myself 50 years younger."[11] He would love to advise his younger self on mistakes to avoid in life.

Baseball great Reggie Jackson felt the same way. "Yes, I would like a Reggie Jackson 2nd because then I could tell the guy not to be a mess for the first 25 years," he said.

But how would the Dawkins or Jackson clone feel about this old guy who was always bothering him with advice and stories about "When I was your age . . . ?" Would the clone listen, or would he resent the advice?

Of course, you can't answer such questions. Since there never have been any human clones, no one can. But it is conceivable that cloning might impose difficult and, in some cases, intolerable psychological burdens on a clone.

Inevitably any discussion of cloning becomes part of a larger discussion of the ethics of all forms of genetic manipulation. In the future it might be possible to eliminate certain inherited diseases by genetic manipulation. It might also be possible to manipulate not only sex, but skin color, height, and a host of other inherited characteristics—in short, to produce "designer babies." Would this be ethical? Might it not eventually lead to the sort of horrors perpetrated by the Nazis in the name of eugenics, or selective breeding? That was Ruth Westheimer's nightmare. Would it not turn babies into products—like prize cattle or sheep? And would the genetically less desirable then be eliminated?

Finally there is what has been called the "yuck factor," or what Kass more grandly terms "the wisdom of repugnance." Most of us just have the feeling that cloning human beings is wrong, it's creepy and revolting, even if we can't explain exactly why. It's something human beings shouldn't do, like cannibalism. It's hard to construct a completely rational argument against cannibalism, particularly if you are starving. But it's something that we don't do—at least most of us don't.

Hold on, say those who favor continued unrestricted research into human cloning. Arguments like that generate more heat than light. Many of the objections raised about possible misuse of cloning fall into the realm of science fiction.

Legally a human clone would be a full human being, just as twins and triplets are all full human beings though they have identical genes with other individuals. Both legally and morally, clones would not be used for providing biological spare parts any more than twins are, or children who are genetically similar to their parents.

As for attempts to create some sort of master race through cloning, advocates for continued research point to sperm banks, stocked with frozen sperm labeled with the IQs and other attributes of the donors. Women have not been lining up at the doors of such institutions to become impregnated this way and thus produce "superior" children. Is there any reason to think it would be different if human cloning becomes available?

Writing in *Reason* magazine contributing editor Ronald Bailey asks rhetorically: "What about a rich jerk who is so narcissistic that he wants to clone himself so that he can give all his wealth to himself? His clone is simply not the same person that he is. The clone may be a jerk too, but he will be his own individual jerk. Nor is Jerk Sr.'s action unprecedented. Today, rich people, and regular people too, make an effort to pass along some wealth to their children when they die.

People will their estates to their children not only because they are connected by bonds of love but also because they have genetic ties. The principle is no different for clones."[12]

Besides, say those who oppose bans on human cloning, the bans won't work anyway. Dr. H. Tristam Engelhardt, a professor of medicine at Baylor University and a philosopher at Rice University, observes there is no reason to think that laws against human cloning would make much difference. "It's such a simple technology, it won't be ban-able. That's why God made offshore islands, so that anybody who wants to do it can have it done." The result of a legal ban on cloning research might simply drive the work underground where it would be practiced without legal oversight.

Secret laboratories cloning human beings? That sounds a bit like the scenario from David Rorvik's cloning hoax or, even worse, from the novel *The Boys from Brazil*.

In December 1997, just as the cloning controversy seemed to be simmering down a bit, an eccentric Chicago scientist announced that he had plans to clone children for infertile couples. Moreover, he said, if cloning were to be banned in the United States he would start his project in some other country where the research was not banned. The scientist, Dr. Richard Seed, had actually been trained as a physicist. He had no institutional connections, no major funding, and was widely regarded as an eccentric. His chances of actually doing what he proposed were virtually nonexistent. Yet his announcement of a project that will almost certainly never begin made front page news all over the country and was at the top of all of the network TV news shows. As when the birth of Dolly was first announced, experts weighed in on both sides. In Congress there was a renewed push to quickly pass a ban on all forms of human cloning research. The effort failed, but more anti-cloning legislation is sure to be introduced.

As you can see the cloning controversy is not over. It has hardly begun. Cloning may well become the great moral, ethical, religious, legal, and scientific controversy that kicks off the beginning of the next millennium.

# CHAPTER 4

# THE FRANKENSTEIN FACTOR

We human beings are an adventurous species, not just physically but intellectually. We like new places, new inventions, new ideas. And yet we are also profoundly conservative. We like what is familiar, what is tried and true. We fear the unknown and we fear knowing too much or going too far. We are proud of ourselves, and yet pride is considered a deadly sin.

A post-Dolly survey found that three out of four Americans felt that human cloning was contrary to the will of God. Yet America has not moved to ban human cloning experiments outright.

These contradictions in human thinking can be found in mythology and religion from earliest times. Look at the ancient Greek legend of Prometheus. There are many different versions of the legend, but the most widely repeated is this one:

Prometheus was a demigod, or Titan, who stole the secret of fire from the chief god Zeus and gave it to the human race. Prometheus was punished for this defiance by being chained to a rock for eternity. Every day an eagle would swoop down and eat Prometheus's liver, which would regenerate overnight so the punishment could be repeated the following day.

The Greek gods had a well-deserved reputation for devising unique and ghastly punishments for those who defied their will. So on the one hand Prometheus's fate stands as a warning to all who would defy the will of the gods, and bring forbidden knowledge, in this case knowledge of the use of fire, to the human race.

On the other hand Prometheus was viewed as a hero, a great figure who risked all to bring this gift of knowledge to humanity. It is Zeus and not Prometheus who is cast as the villain. In later versions the legend is softened by having the hero Hercules free Prometheus from his eternal torment.

The story of Genesis in the Bible tells how Adam and Eve were expelled from the Garden of Eden for giving in to the temptation to know too much. Throughout the world's beliefs, myths, and legends there are many other tales of the terrible fate of those who sought "forbidden knowledge." In order to gain this sort of knowledge the legendary Dr. Faust made a deal with the Devil—with predictably ghastly results.

But of all the figures who are supposed to have suffered because of the search for forbidden knowledge the best known today is Dr. Frankenstein. It is a name that comes up regularly in all discussions of the ethics of cloning, because the secret Dr. Frankenstein sought was the secret of the creation of life itself. That is the most forbidden of all forbidden knowledge.

The Frankenstein myth began in the imagination of an eighteen-year-old English girl, Mary Shelley. She was the brand-new wife of the famous poet Percy Bysshe Shelley. In the summer of 1816 the couple was vacationing in Switzerland. They were living near a villa rented by another famous Englishman, the poet Lord Byron, and visited with him frequently.

The summer was rainy and in order to pass the time Byron suggested that each of them write a ghost story. Mary Shelley came up with the idea for Frankenstein. She was inspired by overhearing a conversation between her husband and Byron about "the nature of the principle of life, and whether there was any probability of its ever being discovered and communicated."

That night she dreamed of ". . . the pale student of unhallowed arts kneeling beside the thing he had put together. I saw the hideous phantasm of a man stretched out, and then . . ."

The story began with a dream but Mary Shelley didn't just sit down and write the book in a creative frenzy. It took her months of hard work, and much rewriting. It took many months more before a publisher could be found, despite the best efforts of Shelley, who was well known in literary circles. In the end the only publisher who would risk putting out such a work was not quite respectable, and specialized in sensationalist literature.

The book was published anonymously, though the name of the author was no secret to Shelley's many literary friends and was quickly revealed to the public at large. Many of the reviewers didn't like the book because they believed it was improper for a young woman to write or even think of such things.

Despite *Frankenstein*'s decidedly mixed critical reception the book proved to be enormously popular and has remained constantly in print since the day of its publication. Its lush, nineteenth-century gothic/romantic prose, and its characters who are always turning pale, clutching at their throats, and fainting, do not appeal to the modern reader. It's too long on talk and description, too short on action. But it does capture the imagination—this is the tale of a man who overstepped the bounds of what we should know, created life, and then was punished by having his monstrous creation turn on him in the most horrible way.

Mary Shelley was not just writing a monster story; she was well aware of the parallels between her Frankenstein who had ventured into forbidden areas of knowledge and the mythical Prometheus. She subtitled her book *The Modern Prometheus*. Percy Shelley had already written a verse play on the subject of Prometheus.

Within a few years after the book was published there were adaptations of it on the stage that were probably more popular than the book itself. After seeing an early production Mary Shelley wrote, "I was much amused, but lo and behold I found myself famous. *Frankenstein* had prodigious success as a drama . . ."

The movies made Mary Shelley's creation more popular than ever, and are more responsible than anything else for imprinting the image of Frankenstein and his monster on the public imagination of the twentieth century.

The first-known film version was made by the Edison Company in 1910, practically at the dawn of the movie industry. And *Frankenstein* has been the basis of more films than any other single work of fiction in history. Whether as a pure horror film, a gothic romance, or a moral tale, the story still speaks to us.

The 1931 Universal Studio's version of the novel, starring Boris Karloff as the monster, is the best and certainly the most famous of the many screen adaptations. It's the film version, not the book, that everybody remembers today, because few people read the book anymore.

In the book, Victor Frankenstein had been a brilliant young student of the natural sciences and son of a respectable civil servant. He receives the "secret" of creating life in a sudden flash of inspiration. In the film he becomes a baron, a nobleman, and a "doctor"—the archetypical white-coated mad scientist. In the film there is a good deal said and shown about robbing graves for body parts that are stitched together to make the monster. Such practices are only briefly and delicately hinted at in the novel.

In March 1972, Willard Gaylin, a psychiatrist and ethicist who believed, prematurely as it turned out, that science stood on the verge of human cloning, wrote an impassioned article for *The New York Times Magazine* titled, "The Frankenstein Myth Becomes a Reality—We Have the Awful Knowledge to Make Exact Copies of Human Beings."[1]

In the many post-Dolly discussions about the limits of science it was the film Frankenstein that was referred to more often than not, usually inadvertently. *New York*

"Keep him here until I return," orders Dr. Frankenstein, Jr.,
in the third Frankenstein film, *Son of Frankenstein*. Basil
Rathbone plays the doctor. Ygor, the shepherd, is played
by Bela Lugosi and Boris Karloff is the monster.

*Times* columnist William Safire wrote of "the creation of Dolly, the lamb formed by cellular biologists in Scotland and fused into life by electric shock as was the Monster in Mary Shelley's *Frankenstein.*"[2] Wrong. It was the movie that had that wonderful scene of the castletop laboratory with the crackling static electric generators and the lightning crashing all around. In Mary Shelley's novel the moment of creation is barely described, and the best the reader can make out from the sketchy details is that Frankenstein used some sort of chemical process—not electricity. Electricity was barely known in Mary Shelley's day.

It doesn't matter anymore. "Dr." Frankenstein, with his white coat and fantastical laboratory, has become part of our culture. He is everybody's vision of the mad scientist. The man who in the pursuit of knowledge goes too far and ventures into territory that should be reserved for God alone. In this case he was searching for the secret to life—and he found it—with the predictably horrible consequences.

Shelley's character Victor Frankenstein had serious doubts about what he was doing. "When I found so astonishing a power placed within my hands I hesitated a long time. I doubted at first whether I should attempt the creation of a being like myself or one of simpler organization." A sheep perhaps?

In the end Frankenstein cannot help but take on the supreme challenge, creating an artificial human being. Incidentally, the creation of Shelley's novel is not the nearly mute and stumbling monster of the film. This creature talks, and talks, and talks. The creature of the novel spends a great deal of time speculating unhappily on the nature of life.

"Dr." Frankenstein himself is drawn from older images of the alchemists. These curious figures are best known today for their attempts to make gold from lead or other base metals. But the alchemists conducted experiments in many areas, including attempts to find the elixir of immortality and create life itself. Depending on the time and place, they might either have received great wealth and honors, or been burned at the stake.

Mary Shelley may have developed her character from stories she had been told about a seventeenth-century German alchemist named Konrad Dippel. Dippel was actually born at a real Castle Frankenstein, a castle owned by the Frankenstein family outside of the German city of Darmstadt. During his life Dippel claimed that he had discovered the secret to living a long life. A year after he made that announcement he died.

Another literary mad scientist who is carrying out dreadful experiments, this time on a remote and secret island, is the character of Dr. Moreau in *The Island of Doctor Moreau* by H. G. Wells. He is creating creatures that are half-human, half-animal. Once again he is tinkering with life and upsetting the natural order of things, with horrible and unforeseen results.

Wells's title character utters the creed of all mad scientists of fiction: "To this day I have never troubled about the ethics of the matter," the doctor says. "The study of Nature makes a man at last as remorseless as

Nature. I have gone on, not heeding anything but the question I was pursuing . . ."

Generation after generation of Hollywood mad scientists have raved, "The world thought me mad. But now I have showed them all," generally followed by an outburst of maniacal laughter.

In Wells's book and in the first film version of the book, which was retitled, *The Island of Lost Souls* (1933), the doctor creates his "manimals" through surgery. In the 1977 film version, the mad Dr. Moreau has switched to genetic manipulation.

In 1932, when Aldous Huxley wrote *Brave New World,* he didn't use the word cloning. He called it "bokanovskification." This was a process used to mass-produce drones for performing manual labor. Huxley's Gammas, Deltas, and Epsilons were separated from the higher-class Alphas and Betas not only by economic status, but also by biologically engineered physical and intellectual traits.

Lots of science-fiction writers from Ray Bradbury to Ursula Le Guin explored the usually grim consequences of cloning in their stories and novels—but no one had a darker vision than Philip K. Dick. Dick's book *Do Androids Dream of Electric Sheep?* was the basis for the film *Blade Runner* (1982). In the world of the future, synthetic human life can be manufactured wholesale. Ethical and moral considerations have disappeared and corporations do a brisk business in "skin jobs," producing and selling concubines, performers, mercenaries, and humanoid pets.

The point is that those who have thought about the ability to create life to order believed it would bring out all of our worst instincts. While science-fiction writers have been optimistic about the future of many other scientific developments, the possibility of cloning is a subject that appears to have only depressed them.

Mass cloning hasn't been the only fear explored by science-fiction writers. Re-creating a specific person can create all sorts of problems. In Ben Bova's novel *Multiple Man* (1976), several exact copies of the U.S. president are found dead and no one is certain whether a clone or the real McCoy sits in the Oval Office. In Nancy Freedman's 1973 book *Joshua, Son of None*, the clone is a real President John F. Kennedy. And then there is one of the most famous cloning novels of all, Ira Levin's *The Boys from Brazil*, in which a fugitive Nazi scientist is trying to clone a flock of little Hitlers in his secret laboratory in Brazil. The 1978 film gave Levin's tale an even wider audience.

If cloning became common, then reproduction—along with male and female genders—would be unnecessary. That's the premise behind books such as Charles Eric Maine's *World Without Men* (1958) and Poul Anderson's *Virgin Planet* (1959).

A more benign view is presented in the British writer Fay Weldon's novel *The Cloning of Joanna May*. It's about a man who dumps his unfaithful wife, but only after cloning her so he can replace her with her twin a few years down the line. The novel was popular enough to be the basis for a BBC miniseries aired in 1992.

In the film *Creator* (1985), Peter O'Toole plays an eccentric Nobel laureate who is trying to make a facsimile of his dead wife to keep him company in his old age.

Actor/director Woody Allen didn't take the potential dangers of cloning too seriously in his 1973 film *Sleeper*. In one scene, Allen's character kidnaps the severed nose of the world dictator before it can be cloned to oppress the world once more, and holds it hostage at gunpoint.

Just a few months before the announcement about Dolly the film *Multiplicity* was released. The comedy starred Michael Keaton as an overworked construction foreman who replicates himself with the help of a local geneticist. The first clone is a macho overachiever, the second an effeminate New Man, and the third (the clone of a clone) a blithering idiot, whose condition is explained in the line, "You know when you make a copy of a copy it is not quite as sharp as the original." *Multiplicity* did not fare well at the box office. If it had been released after the announcement of Dolly it might have found a much larger audience.

In the 1988 film *Twins*, Arnold Schwarzenegger and Danny DeVito play twin brothers—the results of a genetic experiment gone haywire. The DeVito character calls himself "genetic trash."

As soon as the announcement of the cloning of Dolly was made, several production companies rushed cloning films into production. In general these early productions were quickly and cheaply made, and they helped to reinforce the darkly sinister view of human cloning. Humor had not worked very well. The scary side of cloning was what a fearful public wanted.

Films like *Invasion of the Body Snatchers* (1956) and its 1993 remake titled simply *Body Snatchers* and *Species* (1995) are not strictly about cloning. But they leave the viewers with the uncomfortable feeling that exact replicas of humans, even of people we know, can in reality be soulless aliens.

In *Alien Resurrection* (1997), Sigourney Weaver returns as the clone of Ripley, a popular character that she played in earlier films in the series. Here cloning is used simply as a gimmick to bring back characters that were supposed to have died in a previous film. With heightened interest in cloning it is a gimmick that will undoubtedly be used more often in future films to bring back both heroes and monsters who capture the fancy of the audience.

Along with conspiracies and alien abductions cloning has been one of the regular themes of the enormously popular *X-Files* television series. "Eve," one of the earliest episodes, concerns a cloning experiment gone horribly wrong. The female clones, "the Eves," are homicidally psychotic and possess enormous powers.

During the deliberations of the National Bioethics Advisory Committee one of the commissioners, Diane Scott-Jones, a Temple University psychology professor, said that she had recently seen an *X-Files* episode that depicted an army of cloned, mindless agricultural workers. She thought that in the popular imagination cloning represented the "fear of powerful people who can control people who are not at all powerful."

But the biggest use of cloning in popular culture (literally) was in the monumental blockbuster book and film, *Jurassic Park,* and its sequel (some would say clone), *The Lost World: Jurassic Park*. We will look at that subject in detail in the next chapter.

The message of the books and films is always the same—don't go too far. That message made its way right into a famous TV commercial about margarine that is supposed to be so much like butter that it annoys the creator of butter. "It's *not nice* to fool Mother Nature!" says the character in an angry tone amid flashes of lightning and the roar of thunder. That became a popular catch phrase of the day.

Does this sort of entertainment create our fears, or simply reflect them? In one form or another that is an argument that goes on constantly. Certainly our fears are reinforced by what we read and what we see—even if it's only fiction.

# CHAPTER 5

# CLONING
# DINOSAURS

It wasn't the birth of Dolly the sheep that first made cloning a household word in the 1990s, it was *Jurassic Park*.

The average person has little real interest in cloned sheep—which do exist—but is tremendously interested in cloned dinosaurs—which don't exist.

Michael Crichton's 1990 book *Jurassic Park*, which is all about cloning dinosaurs for an amusement park, was a huge best-seller. Stephen Spielberg's even more popular film adapted from the book was released in 1993. At the time, the movie version of *Jurassic Park* was the most phenomenally successful motion picture in history.

It was the second-highest-grossing film in the United States ever, taking in some 357 million dollars at the box office. Worldwide it did even better, with a total of 556 million dollars, making it the number-one-grossing film ever produced, until *Titanic* in 1998.

The sequel (based on Crichton's sequel) *The Lost World: Jurassic Park*, released in the summer of 1997, did not quite equal the popularity of the original, but it too became one of the highest-grossing films in history. It was certainly the most financially successful movie sequel ever made.

The theme of both of these films is the ever-popular man meets man-eating dinosaur. But the reason that we are discussing the subject here is because the dinosaurs were supposed to have been produced in the modern world by cloning. As in most other cloning science fiction the experiment goes horribly wrong.

Dinosaurs have always been popular, and writers of science fiction and makers of science-fiction films have long struggled with the problem of getting humans and dinosaurs together at the same time and in the same place. They have sometimes ignored the facts entirely and made "cave men" and dinosaurs contemporaries. They have found dinosaurs still alive on remote islands or in impenetrable jungles. They have "awakened" frozen dinosaurs with atomic explosions and even found dinosaurs in outer space. Cloning dinosaurs was just the latest, and certainly the most successful, attempt to solve the problem. But is it any more realistic than finding dinosaurs alive and well in a swamp in the center of Africa?

The idea of dinosaur cloning did not entirely spring from the imagination of writers of fiction and makers of movies. Good science fiction is generally based on

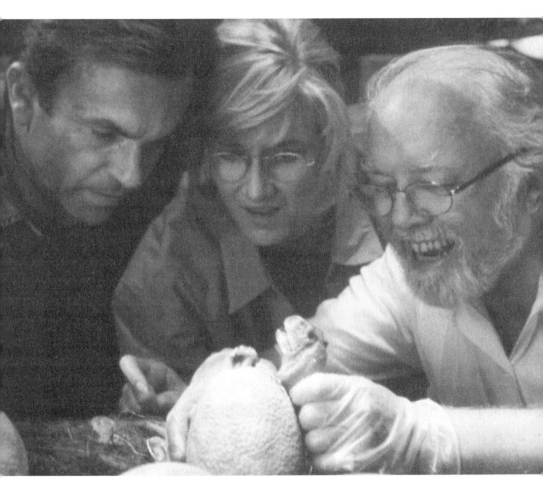

A still from the movie *Jurassic Park*. This movie captured
the imagination of the general public much the way the
concept of a great big dinosaur theme park captured the
imagination of the mastermind in the movie, played by
Richard Attenborough.

real science, or what the public believes to be real science. In the early 1980s a Canadian scientist named Charles Pellegrino suggested that it might be possible to clone dinosaurs or other long-extinct creatures through the recovery and use of ancient DNA.

The richest source for such material, he said, might be from ancient insects preserved in amber. Amber is fossilized tree sap. It's quite hard, usually has a rich yellow color, and is often used in jewelry. Occasionally a small creature, like an insect, has been found inside of a piece of amber. At some time the insect was trapped and encased in the sap while it was still liquid. The sap then dried, hardened, and fossilized into a glossy yellow lump.

Amber has excellent preservative qualities. It protects whatever is inside of it from moisture and other elements that would tend to degrade and destroy it. Small wonder that the ancient Egyptians, who knew a thing or two about preservation, used tree resins to embalm their mummies.

Insects, spiders, centipedes, frogs, and the feathers of birds have been found entombed in pieces of amber. The creatures inside the amber are kept in a remarkable state of preservation for hundreds of thousands, even millions, of years. Some insects found trapped and preserved in amber date back to the time of the dinosaurs—65 million or more years ago. We are not talking about imprints here, like fossil footprints, or the imprints of the skeletons of fish found in shale rock. This is the entire organism. George O. Poinar, a paleontologist at the University of California at Berkeley who has done a lot of research in this area, and also lays claim to being the person who inspired Crichton's *Jurassic Park* idea, says, "This is the entire organism that is preserved to the point that we can actually make out cellular structures in exquisite detail, including the nuclei where the genes reside."

Now let us say that a blood-sucking insect living during the Jurassic Period, about 140 million years ago, has just had a meal from a passing dinosaur. Stuffed with dinosaur blood the insect is then unlucky enough to blunder into a sticky sun-warmed dollop of tree sap, becomes trapped, and is covered by sap and suffocates. As time passes the sap turns to amber preserving the insect, but also, in theory, preserving its last meal, the dinosaur blood. The blood contains cells, perhaps thousands of them, and the cells should, or at least might, contain dinosaur DNA.

Now if that dinosaur DNA could be recovered and identified it should give scientists a complete genetic blueprint for a dinosaur. Then, in theory again, the DNA could be used to clone a living dinosaur. That is the premise of *Jurassic Park*.

Other possible sources of dinosaur DNA have been suggested. There has been speculation that dinosaur bone marrow might somehow have survived fossilization and thus still contain DNA. But the DNA in amber-preserved biting insects seemed the best bet in the early 1980s. That's why Crichton used it in his book and why it played a prominent part in the film.

The problem for Pellegrino was that few of his scientific colleagues took such theories seriously. Respected scientific journals refused to print his articles on the subject. Finally in frustration he turned to the popular science publication *Omni,* which often prints highly speculative, even sensational, science-oriented pieces. At first his article "Dinosaur Capsule," outlining the possibilities of recovering dinosaur DNA and cloning dinosaurs, didn't get much response. "Looking back, I wonder if anyone except Michael Crichton ever read it. But does it matter? He was enough," said Pellegrino later.

He continued, "With Crichton's novel, *Jurassic Park,* and Spielberg's subsequent phenomenally successful film adaptation, science fiction once again made complex scientific ideas respectable. What Jules Verne did for submarines, what Robert Heinlein and Arthur C. Clarke did for translunar flights, Crichton and Spielberg did for the emerging science of paleogenics [ancient genetics]. All that remains is for the realities of scientific achievement to once again catch up with the fiction."[1]

In his first article Pellegrino predicted that it would take about thirty years for the technology necessary to make the cloning of dinosaurs at least thinkable. Ten years later he said that science was right on schedule, and that we could begin thinking seriously about the subject in another twenty years. That is a rather fuzzy prediction, for there can be a very long gap between thinking seriously about a goal and actually being able to accomplish that goal. And not all serious thoughts turn out to be realistic.

Yet when we see the incredibly realistic-looking dinosaurs that flash and lumber across the screen in *Jurassic Park,* we get the feeling that these things really can be resurrected. With the newly announced advances in cloning and other forms of advanced genetic research we may even begin to believe that such developments are right around the corner.

But hold on, there is still a huge chasm between the practical workaday world of the Roslin Institute and *Jurassic Park*. Dolly is a sheep, not a dinosaur.

The first question that must be answered is: Has dinosaur DNA in any form actually survived the millennia? The answer is that we simply do not know. Most scientists doubt that it has. The insect would have to have become covered with tree sap and die almost immediately after ingesting the dinosaur blood. Otherwise the insect would begin to digest the blood and any DNA it might contain would be destroyed by the digestive enzymes. Just how long this might take is unknown, but the time would be measured in minutes not hours. In fact, to date, no suitable amber-preserved biting insect from the age of the dinosaurs has ever been identified. That doesn't means such specimens don't exist, but if they do they are going to be very, very rare.

Did dinosaur blood cells contain a full complement of DNA? Some animal blood cells don't. Human red blood cells don't. The blood cells of a bird do contain all the necessary DNA. Dinosaurs are not closely related to us, and they may be close relatives of birds. But the fact remains that we know nothing about the structure of dinosaur blood cells, and it takes a leap of faith to assume that they had all the dinosaur DNA.

In order to test amberized insects for dinosaur DNA today, with our still primitive procedures, the specimens would have to be destroyed in the process. Pellegrino notes "compared to the microsurgical techniques that we will need to ferret out dinosaur DNA, it is like trying to figure out how an antique watch worked by smashing it open with a sledgehammer." Searching for dinosaur genes with present-day technology is "out of the question," he insists.[2]

Rob DeSalle, a curator at the American Museum of Natural History in New York, and David Lindley, a science writer, seriously discussed the many problems involved in "building" a dinosaur in their 1997 book *The Science of Jurassic Park and The Lost World*. They concluded that the possibility of finding dinosaur DNA inside a blood-sucking insect preserved in amber was extremely remote. "Sadly, here is a lesson that every scientist learns, and usually pretty quickly; it's easy to have clever ideas, but it's rare to have clever ideas that actually work."[3]

They suggest another possible source of dinosaur DNA, a piece of a dinosaur itself, preserved in amber. Now obviously no one expects to find a whole dinosaur, even an extremely small one preserved in amber. Not all dinosaurs were giants. Some were no bigger than chickens, but there were no mosquito-sized dinosaurs. But what if a couple of dinosaurs got into a fight, probably over the attempt of one dinosaur to eat the other? Dinosaurs would almost certainly be messy eaters, and during the meal chunks of dinosaur flesh might be flying every which way. The same sort of thing might happen when a dead dinosaur was devoured by scavengers, often other dinosaurs. One or more of these chunks might be flung into a tree and land in a glob of resin, which would then harden into amber.[4]

---

The salamander encased in this amber
appears to be so perfectly preserved that it
is not such a stretch of the imagination to
imagine it being cloned by today's
technology.  One only needs to begin to
think through the problem, however, before
realizing the impossibilities.

No such amber-encased dinosaur flesh has ever been found, or at least not identified. There is no way of figuring the odds on whether such material even exists. But it is no less likely than finding the dinosaur blood inside of the preserved insect.

Then comes the problem of identifying the dinosaur DNA. We don't even know what dinosaur DNA is supposed to look like. Scientists can imagine a series of tests that could be used to identify possible dinosaur DNA, but with current technology such tests would be enormously time consuming and expensive. These are not just minor "technical" problems. And in the end the tests might not work.

Charles Pellegrino now believes that there may be another richer and much more expendable and more obvious source of dinosaur DNA on the horizon—fossil dinosaur bones. When he had first speculated about the possible preservation of ancient DNA he thought that some DNA might be found in fossilized dinosaur bones, though he did not think that to be very likely. During the fossilization process all organic matter is leached out of the bones and replaced by other minerals. Fossilized "bones" are not really bones at all, but inorganic minerals that have retained the shape of the original bones. That something as delicate as DNA might somehow have survived this process seemed almost unbelievable.

Then in 1994 stories began to surface indicating that dinosaur DNA somehow miraculously has survived in fossilized bones. Scott R. Woodward of Brigham Young University reported that he had detected pieces of DNA from dinosaur bones estimated to be 80 million years old. But other researchers later contended that what had been found was human DNA that had contaminated the original tests. One of the critics said, "Human DNA is probably the most common laboratory contaminant. It's exceedingly difficult to keep human tissue out of an experiment, because specks of dust have human skin and hair on them."

There were other reports of the discovery of ancient DNA, not just from dinosaurs but from ancient plants and other once-living things. Within months newly developed and more sensitive tests threw grave doubts on these findings. The DNA found in the ancient sources was more likely a contaminant from soil or groundwater that had been in contact with the fossil.

Jeffrey Bada of Scripps Institution of Oceanography, who developed the tests, said he doubted if DNA could survive for more than a few thousand years in temperate climates, and perhaps 100,000 years in cold climates like Alaska or Antarctica. That is a long way from the 65 million years that have passed since the final dinosaur breathed its last.

The only exception might be the DNA from insects or possibly the pieces of dinosaur steak preserved in amber. The tests found that DNA could survive there for at least 130 million years. "Amber is just a great medium for preserving stuff," Bada said. "It's waterproof, and when you get water out of a system you have very little degradation."[5]

OK, let's imagine for the moment that scientists have been able to locate and identify dinosaur DNA. Does that solve the problem? No, an even more formidable obstacle remains. In order to be used for cloning the recovered DNA would have to be absolutely perfect. Remember that Dolly was cloned from the nucleus of a cell taken from living tissue. Even in the science-fiction world of *Jurassic Park* the notion of completely intact dinosaur genes was rejected. In the book and film the dino DNA was "reconstructed." It is possible to reconstruct partial or damaged DNA, but it isn't easy. And that is reconstructing DNA of a known species. Once again, we don't know what dinosaur DNA was like. We have no model. Trying to reconstruct it would be largely guesswork, and if there is just one tiny little wrong guess, you don't have a dinosaur.

It is not unduly pessimistic to state that given current technology or any technology that can be reasonably envisioned in the near future it would be impossible to reconstruct dinosaur DNA.

If the DNA itself doesn't survive from the age of the dinosaurs some protein molecules from dinosaurs may have. Researchers at Montana State University's Museum of the Rockies, one of the premier dinosaur research facilities in the world, have located some curious-looking structures in a slice of *Tyrannosaurus rex* bone. They believe that what they have found may be remnants of the dinosaur's red blood cells, and may contain dinosaur protein. To date, a variety of sensitive tests have not proved this claim—but the tests have not disproved it either, so the researchers remain hopeful.

Now a few ancient protein molecules from a dinosaur are not going to provide the kind of material that can be used to clone a *T. rex* anytime soon, if ever. However, what such molecules may do—assuming they are the real thing—is provide some information about the origins of dinosaurs, and their relationship to modern animals. They might, for example, help to resolve the long-running controversy over whether modern birds are descended from dinosaurs, or if the dinosaurs were more closely related to modern reptiles like alligators.

While this information would be of great interest to paleontologists and a dinosaur-obsessed public, it would bring us no closer to the living dinosaur clones of *Jurassic Park*. But if we learned more about the dinosaurs' evolutionary relationship to modern animals that could help scientists construct a possible model for dinosaur DNA. But that is a long, long way down the road.

For a moment, let us sweep all of these irritating and disappointing objections aside and simply assume that complete dinosaur DNA could be recovered. Now we face another problem: Where would the dinosaur embryo develop? *Jurassic Park* mentions incubation in plastic eggs in a hot, misty "Jurassic atmosphere." It sounds scientific, but it's really just science-fiction technobabble.

Remember now, with Dolly and with frogs, a cell nucleus was inserted into an egg—a sheep egg in the case of the sheep, a frog egg in the case of a frog,—in order to produce a clone. We don't have any dinosaur eggs, at least none that have not already been turned to useless stone by the fossilization process. What is needed to clone a baby dinosaur is a mommy dinosaur, and we don't have any mommy dinosaurs. We don't have any close living relatives of the dinosaurs. We don't even know who the closest living relatives of the dinosaurs are. Are they crocodiles or ostriches? And if we did know, we can't be sure that any modern relative of the dinosaur would be of any help in cloning.

The small band of optimists believe that the obstacles are mere technical bumps in the road that can be overcome by research and experiment in the next few decades. And perhaps the optimists are right. Scientific progress has proved surprisingly difficult to predict. Sometimes advances can be remarkable, and things once deemed impossible become commonplace. But these technical problems are enormous. They will not be easily overcome. The disappointing conclusion is that you probably won't be seeing living, breathing dinosaurs in a zoo or amusement park in your lifetime. Be content with those very lifelike dinosaurs on the movie and TV screens and probably as robots. Technological advances in these areas are almost certain, and those dinosaurs will look more alive than ever in the future.

If cloned dinosaurs are out of the question, how about cloning something a little more recent—like a woolly mammoth? That may be a lot more practical. Mammoths have been found frozen in the permafrost of Siberia and Alaska. These creatures lived during the Pleistocene era, which was tens of thousands rather than tens of millions of years ago. Well-preserved specimens, not just fossils, have been discovered over the years, and there are certainly more of them out there. Such specimens may contain intact woolly mammoth DNA. Embryos might be grown in eggs extracted from a modern elephant, a close relative of the extinct woolly mammoth.[6]

Once again, any such attempt would encounter a host of daunting technical problems, and in the end might prove to be impossible. But the prospect of Pleistocene Park is a whole lot more realistic than the prospect of Jurassic Park.

## CHAPTER 6

# GENETIC ENGINEERING

When a journalist asked Nobel-prizewinning biologist James Watson about the Roslin Institute's accomplishment of cloning an adult sheep, the famed scientist sounded unimpressed.

"This could have been done in 1938. It's moving cells, not DNA." Cloning, Watson and others have always insisted, is fairly easy. The next step is genetic engineering, actually moving DNA, and the debate about cloning inevitably becomes entwined with the ongoing debate over genetic engineering. This involves not merely producing a twin or multiple twins of an individual but actually changing the genetic makeup of that individual.

As Dr. Ian Wilmut pointed out repeatedly during interviews, the aim of his experiments was not really to make more identical sheep but to produce sheep and other animals that had been genetically altered to serve specific purposes. Somehow that point was lost in all the multiple images of Michael Jordan and Albert Einstein.

Yet not so very long ago genetic engineering was the subject of fierce controversy, just as cloning is today. The history of that controversy can help us understand the current cloning controversy, and possibly give us an idea as to how the controversy will finally play out.

DNA—the initials are very nearly as well known as CIA or IRS, and sometimes very nearly as mysterious, powerful, and scary. DNA stands for deoxyribonucleic acid, the substance that holds the blueprint for all life. It is what differentiates a bacterium from a bug, a bug from a bird, and a bird from your brother.

The importance of the DNA molecule as the key to genetics was recognized as early as the 1940s, but it wasn't until 1953 that scientists were actually able to figure out the structure of the DNA. The molecule turned out to be enormously long, a thousand times longer than it is wide. It is made up of two intertwined spiral strands—described by its discoverers as a "double helix."

This discovery was made by Francis Crick, a British physicist who wanted to become involved in biophysical research, and James Watson, a twenty-four-year-old postdoctoral student from the University of Chicago.

The story of the discovery was an important one, and the two discoverers, particularly the brash and outspoken young Watson, were engaging characters. They

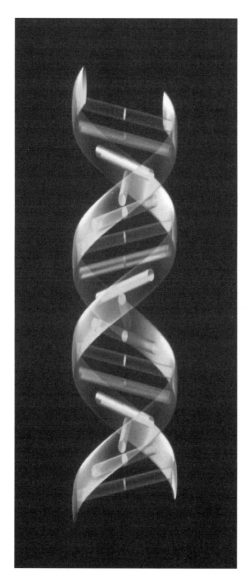

The Watson-Crick double-helix DNA molecule.

won the Nobel Prize in 1962 and Watson wrote an account of the work called *The Double Helix* in 1968, which became a best-seller, a rarity for a nonfiction book about basic science. DNA research got the sort of public attention that is almost never given to basic discoveries in science. If most people didn't exactly know what DNA was, at least they had heard of it and knew that it was important.

Simply determining the structure of DNA was, of course, not the end of the road. Scientists began to experiment with ways of manipulating DNA. By the early 1970s researchers had found ways of splitting apart a DNA molecule and recombining it with DNA from an entirely different molecule. Molecular biologists could create genetic combinations that had never been seen in nature. This was called recombinant DNA.

Recombinant DNA represented a tremendous advance in genetics. But would this new knowledge be used for good or evil? Quite suddenly the field of genetics, which had seemed so benign, particularly when compared with physics, which brought us the atomic bomb, began to seem "unnatural" and downright scary. Phrases like "playing God" began to be heard, and the name of Frankenstein came up regularly in discussions of recombinant DNA.

It wasn't the public that first became alarmed, it was the biologists themselves. They began to realize that it would be possible to insert genes in bacteria that would make them resistant to antibiotics or make them more dangerous in any one of a huge number of ways. That seemed to open the door to the possibility of accidentally creating a germ that could kill everyone. There were an awful lot of new people entering the hot new field of genetics who were not familiar with the disciplined laboratory precautions used by those who study dangerous bacteria. The increase in the number of laboratories handling animal viruses led to a feeling that there was a growing need to consider potential health hazards.

Much of the early work with DNA involved studying the common *E. coli* bacteria found in the intestines of every human being, because its genetic structure was well known and it was comparatively easy to work with. Then in 1971, Janet Mertz, a young microbiologist working in the laboratory of Dr. Paul Berg at Stanford University in California, told a meeting of microbiologists at Cold Spring Harbor on Long Island of an experiment to join the chromosome of a virus that appeared to cause cancer in laboratory rats with a strain of *E. coli*. It was highly improbable that this particular virus could cause cancer in humans; it had originally been discovered in monkeys, where it was harmless. But monkeys and humans are not identical so the production of a new virus causing human cancer was not impossible. The worst case scenario was that a common intestinal bacterium, now engineered so that it could cause cancer in humans, would be unknowingly turned loose on the world. That scared a lot of people.

One of those who heard the Mertz talk, Robert Pollack, who was doing microbiological research at Cold Spring Harbor, was genuinely alarmed. He called Berg, suggesting that the proposed experiments be postponed.

"We're in a pre-Hiroshima situation," he said. "It would be a real disaster if one of the agents now being handled in research should in fact be a real human cancer agent."

At first Berg seemed to think that such concerns were exaggerated. But he talked to his colleagues and found they were also worried. Berg changed his mind and the experiment was abandoned. Later, Walter Rowe, a molecular biologist at the National Cancer Institute, remarked, "The Berg experiment scares the pants off a lot of people, including him."

Pretty soon scientists were lining up on both sides of the controversy. Biologist Philip Siekevitz wrote to the journal *Science*: "Are we really that much farther along on the path to comprehensive knowledge that we can forget the overwhelming pride with which Dr. Frankenstein made his monster and the Rabbi of Prague made his Golem? To those who would answer 'Yes,' I would accuse of harboring that sin which the Greeks held to be one of the greatest, that of overweening pride. Like the physicists before us, we have entered the realm of the Faustian bargain, and it behooves all of us biologists to think very carefully about the conditions of these agreements before we plunge ahead into the darkness."[1]

Physicist Freeman Dyson shot back that while there were certainly theoretical dangers in recombinant DNA research, the possible advantages were far too great to be ignored. There was the hope of a cure for cancer, the creation of new food crops that could save millions from starvation, and energy crops that would provide alternatives to polluting fossil fuels and dangerous nuclear energy.

His letter concluded that while there were certainly unknown risks, we should not ignore the fact that there might also be unknown benefits. "It is equally true that the real benefit to humanity from recombinant DNA will probably be the one no one has dreamed of, "Dyson said." Our ignorance lies equally on both sides of the balance. All that we can say with certainty is that prodigious changes in the conditions of human life must come within the next century if civilization is to survive. The exploitation of recombinant DNA is only one of these changes, and perhaps not the most dangerous nor least hopeful."[2]

In February 1975 many of the world's leaders in biological research gathered in Asilomar, California, for a conference on the possible dangers of recombinant DNA research. The conference was confused and often chaotic, but in the end a majority of those present called for stiff guidelines regulating recombinant DNA research. There was a small but eminent minority, including Nobel laureate James Watson, who insisted that there were no special dangers in the research so no special precautions or guidelines were necessary. Watson and his supporters saw great potential harm in what they described as overregulating scientific research. The view held by Watson and his colleagues did not carry the day.

By this time the controversy was no longer limited to scientists. The general public had become involved. Legislation was introduced in Congress to restrict and carefully oversee recombinant DNA research. The city council of Cambridge, Massachusetts, home of Harvard University and the Massachusetts Institute of Technology, voted for a temporary moratorium on such research. Restrictive legislation was introduced in California. The issue became a major focus for the growing environmental movement, which feared the creation of a whole new class of threats to the environment from genetically altered pesticides or from other agricultural products.

It was the author Michael Crichton who had inadvertently crystallized people's fears in his 1969 novel *The Andromeda Strain*, which was made into a popular movie in 1970. In the book an unknown microorganism, picked up in space, is brought back to Earth by a satellite that crashes in New Mexico. There are also hints that the germ may have something to do with biological warfare experiments.

In any case, this new and rapidly mutating microorganism kills off nearly everyone in a small New Mexico town, and looks to be well on its way to creating a worldwide plague. Though both the book and the film predate the recombinant DNA controversy, the phrase Andromeda Strain became a common description of the sort of thing that could be released on an unsuspecting human race by such research.

Once the controversy became public there was a rush of films and books that exploited the most horrifying potentials of DNA research. Dr. Lewis Thomas, writing in the *New England Journal of Medicine* lamented: ". . . here we are, caught up in a public controversy in which the only issue being talked about seems to be the invention of monsters for their own sake, mini-Frankensteins, and it is even being made to seem as though this is really how investigators engaged in work of this kind obtain their pleasure, like the mad scientists in their basement laboratories in grade B movies . . . the workers in this field are not about to manufacture hybrid beings. They are trying to find out how things work."[3]

But much of the general public simply did not trust the goodwill and good sense of scientists. A much more common attitude was summed up by *San Francisco Chronicle* columnist Charles McCabe in a column dated April 4, 1977. McCabe began by describing scientists as "Those lovely people who gave us the atom bomb . . ." He went on to admit that he didn't understand DNA research, but that one thing he did understand was that it was "an act of creation" and that it "scares the day-lights out of me."

"Jiggling with genes may cure cancer. Then again, it may cause outbreaks of new forms of cancer. Gene-splicing may clean up spills and at the same time might defoliate half a state.

"Who knows? The only thing that is certain about this business is that nobody knows. Even molecular bi-ologists, whose racket it is, say that neither the puta-tive good nor harm of DNA recombinant research can be known for years.

"Why, in the name of all that is sacred, can't we learn to let well enough alone? Why do we diddle cease-lessly with nature? Why will scientists persist in play-ing God?"[4]

And then, just as the controversy seemed to be reaching a boiling point, it began to simmer down. It was discovered that DNA transfer also took place in nature, so recombinant DNA was not as "unnatural" as it had once been assumed. Many of those scientists who had first warned of the dangers began to say that upon further reflection, and with greater knowledge, it now appeared that their fears had been exaggerated. The heated disapproval that had greeted all research with recombinant DNA began to fade away. Very few seemed to notice.

In 1980, Paul Berg of Stanford, in whose laboratory the entire controversy was ignited, was one of the winners of the Nobel Prize in chemistry for work with recombinant DNA. Also in 1980, in a five-to-four decision the U.S. Supreme Court voted that "a live, human-made microorganism is patentable subject matter." In other words, forms of life can be patented if there is a man-made element to them. This decision gave a huge boost to the fledgling genetic-engineering industry. Suddenly it seemed as if money, and lots of it, could be made "jiggling with genes." There was some public discomfort over the idea of "patenting" living things. It was the "yuck" factor. The animal rights people objected vigorously to "patenting life." But the momentum and much of the emotion had already gone out of the arguments against genetic engineering.

By 1982 what had once been viewed as a threat became an investment opportunity. Genentech, the first company based on recombinant DNA technology, went public. Wall Street valued the company at $200 million. The Stanford biologists who had founded the company became millionaires.

Genentech was only the first of many new companies based on genetic engineering to be founded over the past two decades, and genetic engineering now represents a large percentage of the research in the pharmaceutical industry.

Today there are a number of genetically altered products, from medicine to agricultural products, on the market. We eat genetically altered vegetables and wear genetically altered cotton, usually without ever being aware of it. There are still some fears of genetically altered super germs, but such fears are concentrated on deliberate genetic alterations for germ warfare, rather than on the accidental release of deadly microorganisms.

Most scientists now look back on the heated controversy over recombinant DNA as unnecessary. While the uses of the technology still remain very much a subject of discussion, the discussions no longer have an apocalyptic tone. Much of what once seemed terribly frightening, immoral, and nearly unthinkable has now become commonplace.

And here is where genetic engineering and the story of Dolly the cloned sheep come together. The research that led to the cloning of Dolly was sponsored by a Scottish company called PPL Therapeutics, Ltd. The company wants to develop a technique in which genes are inserted into the cells of sheep or other farm animals that would force the cells to make substances that could be used as drugs to treat human ailments, like clotting factors for hemophiliacs. The animals cloned from those cells would produce the drugs in their milk. Then the clones could be milked and the drugs extracted. This would be more efficient and much cheaper than the conventional ways of making such drugs.

It should come as no surprise that just about one year after Dolly was born the same Roslin Institute team produced two other cloned sheep called Polly and Molly.

Dolly, on the right, is joined by the world's
first transgenic lamb, named Polly.

The name Polly was drawn from the breed, Poll Dorset lamb. The name Molly was used because it rhymes with the other two names. In a sense Polly and Molly were not as spectacular an achievement as Dolly because they were cloned from fetal rather than adult cells. But Polly and Molly are not just a product of cloning, they are also products of genetic engineering. They contain a human gene. In addition to the human gene, Polly and Molly contain a second innocuous gene added as a marker.

No, the scientists are not trying to create some sort of monstrous human/sheep hybrid. Scientists have been able to genetically alter animals for some time now. This development speeds up the process. The human gene should allow the sheep to produce a blood-clotting protein called Factor IX in their milk. This substance can be lifesaving for hemophiliacs.

In the past adding DNA was hit or miss. It would only work in about one out of one hundred animals. Only after an animal was born were scientists able to determine if the added genes had been taken up by the embryo cells. That was time consuming, expensive, and inefficient.

With cloning, scientists can now grow cells in the laboratory, drench them with genes, select those few cells that take up the genes, and use them to make clones from those cells. This new method also allows researchers to selectively remove or suppress particular genes, another big step in genetic engineering.

While scientists expected such developments eventually, they are coming much faster than most had predicted. Dr. Lee Silver, a molecular geneticist at Princeton

University, said, "After Dolly, everyone would have predicted this, but they were saying it would happen in 5 or 10 years."

And he added hopefully, or ominously depending on your point of view, "We are getting closer and closer to human beings now, too. All of this can be passed over to human beings. Genetic engineering of human beings is now really on the horizon."[5]

## CHAPTER 7

# THE FUTURE

THE FUTURE

Before we plunge more deeply into speculation about the future of cloning, a few cautionary tales from history would be useful. The road of scientific and technological progress is not smooth, straight, or always predictable. Sometimes developments that initially seem not only probable, but absolutely inevitable, do not become reality.

When Neil Armstrong first stepped on the moon in 1969, there were predictions that there would be regular flights to the moon within twenty years. A major airline set up a waiting list for its first commercial flight to the moon and thousands of people scrambled to get on the list. After twenty years had passed the airline had gone out of business and moon landings of any kind seem a distant memory.

In the early 1970s there were confident predictions of huge manned orbiting space stations and manned flights to the planet Mars by the end of the century. Well, the end of the century is almost upon us and what we have is one broken-down Russian space station and a few technically interesting but tiny unmanned flights to Mars.

And we're still waiting for nuclear power to become the source of cheap and abundant energy, as many predicted half a century ago.

The awesome scientific events of the past five decades have been accompanied by equally awesome predictions of their impact in the not-too-distant future. Some came true. Some are still possible. Many were just plain wrong.

A year after the stunning announcement of the birth of Dolly, no other mammal had been successfully cloned from the cells of an adult. In science it is essential that an experiment be repeated successfully to rule out the possibility of fraud or error in the original work. Since the experiment had not been repeated some scientists began to raise criticisms and doubts about the Dolly experiment.

Confirming evidence for the Dolly experiment began to trickle in slowly. Early in 1998—almost exactly two years after Dolly made history—cloned calves were born at a livestock research laboratory in Japan. Other large animals, including cows and sheep, were reported to be pregnant with clones.

Soon Dolly was in the news again. Dr. Wilmut and his associates at the Roslin Institute announced that Dolly the clone had given birth—the old fashioned way—to a perfectly normal sheep. There had been some fears that a clone produced from the cell of a six-year-old animal might, in some way, be aged or damaged. Dolly's normal development appears to have quieted those fears.

The whole issue of cloning slipped out of the news until an explosive announcement in July of 1998. Dr. Ryuzo Yanagimachi, a biologist at the University of Hawaii, and his postdoctoral student Teruhiko Wakayama, published a report in the scientific journal *Nature* on twenty-two mice clones from adult cells, seven of which were clones of clones. In all, they said that they had produced a total of more than fifty mouse clones.

After the *Nature* article was published, there were still a few scientific skeptics, but far less than before. What is more, the technique used by the Hawaiian researchers appears to be simpler and more fool-proof than the technique used to produce Dolly. And with mice, researchers can study and perfect cloning in an easily available and familiar lab animal.

"Wow," said Dr. Barry Zirkin, head of the Division of Reproductive Biology at Johns Hopkins University in Baltimore. "This is going to be Dolly multiplied by 22." And Dr. Lee Silver, a Princeton geneticist, did not flinch from describing the broader implications. "Absolutely we're going to have cloning of humans."

There are still obstacles in creating clones of large animals. The ratio of 277 failures to one success that produced Dolly has so far not been greatly improved, and no one really knows why. There appears to be a variety of reasons why most clones fail to develop successfully. Several researchers have found that clones have a tendency to grow too large in the womb, presenting a significant risk not only to the newborn but to the mother.

"We've had some [cattle calves] that were just monstrous, up to 180 pounds (82 kilograms)" compared with the normal of 80 pounds (36 kilograms), said Mark Westhusin, a veterinary physiologist at Texas A & M University. "We're back here messing around with the first seven days of life and having a dramatic effect 180 days later," he said. "I think it's pretty clear that there are differences in these [cloned] embryos and the genes they're expressing."[1]

But in working with mice, Dr. Yanagimachi appears to have simplified the technique and made it much more routine and reliable. He told interviewers that he could now clone every day with absolutely no difficulty and turn out normal baby mice after an equally normal twenty-day gestation period. The first cloned mouse to survive to adulthood, named Cumulina, was born on October 3, 1997. Many of the clones have since mated and given birth, indicating that they are healthy and reproductively normal.

Researchers continue to look at other ways of cloning. Scientists from Advanced Cell Technology in Amherst, Massachusetts, said that they had used embryo cell cloning techniques to make genetically identical pigs, and had also made transgenic pig clones bearing an extra human gene. The company hoped that they would ultimately be able to grow pigs with "humanized" organs that could be transplanted into people with less risk of rejection.

There was even a suggestion of the future possibility of cloned pets. When a beloved cat or dog dies, a clone of the animal as a lovable kitten or puppy might become available. It would be expensive, but Americans spend more on pet food than on baby food.

Geneti-Pet of Washington State has begun cryogenically freezing and storing blood samples of household pets in anticipation of the day when genetic technology may enable the deceased animals to be cloned. The company won't actually clone the animals, but it will store the blood in liquid nitrogen, where it can be kept in a near-perfect state of preservation at a fee of $200 a year until the time that geneticists will be able to create clones from the blood cells. The company president says that he got the idea from ongoing scientific experiments to save endangered species. He figures the necessary procedures will become common within ten years.

And then there are the monkey clones.

Just a week after the cloning of Dolly became headline news, scientists at the Oregon Regional Primate Research Center said that they had successfully produced two cloned monkeys, named Neti and Ditto. The monkeys were cloned from embryo cells—not from adult cells as was the case with Dolly. The scientists said that their aim was to create genetically identical monkeys for use in research, and that they had no plans to produce cloned monkeys from adults.

Still the implications of successfully cloning a species that is so closely related to humans could not be avoided.

"It demands that we take seriously the issue of human cloning," said Arthur Caplan, a bioethicist at the University of Pennsylvania.[2]

Now with the success the University of Hawaii researchers have had in producing mouse clones, the subject of human cloning is more impossible to avoid than ever. In 1998, some experts were predicting the first human clone within five years.

Though federal funds for research into human cloning had been banned, at least temporarily, the research that produced Neti and Ditto was supported by government grants—and despite the uproar over cloning the funding for this research has not been withdrawn.

When the cloning of Dolly was first announced in February 1997 most scientists, religious leaders, ethicists, and politicians declared that human cloning was something that was unnecessary, and should never be attempted. The news about Dolly had ignited a virtual firestorm of protest and ethical soul-searching. By year's end the fire was out, at least temporarily.

On the front page of the December 2, 1997, edition of *The New York Times,* Gina Kolata, the reporter who had followed the cloning story for many years, wrote: "There has been an enormous change in attitudes in just a few months; scientists have become sanguine about the notion of cloning and, in particular, cloning a human being."

She quotes Lori Andrews, a professor of law at Chicago-Kent College and an expert on legal issues of reproduction, who said, "I absolutely think the tenor has changed. People who said human cloning would never

The rhesus monkey clones.  They were named Neti
(for nuclear embryo transfer infant) and Ditto
(for obvious reasons).

be done are now saying, 'Well the risks aren't that great.' I see a total shift in the burden of proof to saying that unless you can prove there is actually going to be harm then we should allow it." With Dr. Yanagimachi's startling news from Hawaii, the shift in tone has become even more pronounced.

Noted constitutional scholar Professor Laurence Tribe of Harvard University says that people are now asking "whether human cloning isn't just an incremental step beyond what we are already doing with artificial insemination, in vitro fertilization, fertility enhancement drugs and genetic manipulation."

He predicts that this new attitude "is sure to give way before long to yet another wave of prohibitionist outrage." But this time around Professor Tribe says that though he was once an advocate of prohibiting all attempts at human cloning, it is now a position he no longer feels comfortable with.

"If human cloning is to be banned, then, the reasons had better be far more compelling than any thus far advanced."[3]

Dr. Steen Willadsen, who developed some of the techniques that were used to make Dolly, has said it was "just a matter of time" before the first human being is cloned.

Paul Berg, the Nobel laureate from Stanford University, in whose laboratory the great recombinant DNA controversy of the 1970s really began, observed that whenever science comes up with something really new, like gene splicing or cloning, "the first reaction is fear." But Berg said that we have to reflect and look back to see if this initial reaction was correct. He asked rhetorically if we had learned nothing from the tales of super germs escaping from the laboratory and running amuck.

Will the cloning controversy simply fade away as the recombinant DNA controversy did?

Reviewing the apparent changing attitudes toward cloning *New York Times* reporter George Johnson wrote, "Over time, all the dire warnings and predictions seem to have the opposite of the intended effect. People become inured to the predictable hand-wringing and begin to feel that every new development is accompanied by an obligatory round of chilling scenarios, which often turn out to be wrong. Each new pill, for better or worse, is just a little bit easier to swallow. One wonders whether in ten years, or in five or three, the outrage over cloning will seem as misguided as medieval bans on dissecting cadavers in medical schools. What was the big deal, anyway?"[4]

But the cloning controversy may be different from some of the other issues of the past. The recombinant DNA fears were kicked off by scientists themselves who had discovered a new technique, and were genuinely alarmed and unsure of what it might produce. When the facts indicated that many of the fears they had expressed were exaggerated or completely groundless they changed their positions. The public, now reassured that there would be no worldwide epidemics of laboratory-made germs, promptly forgot about the controversy.

Cloning, however, is much more than a scientific controversy; it is an ethical, moral, philosophical, and even legal controversy. It is not merely exaggerated fears of a brave new world with armies of genetically engineered clones, or little Hitler clones being released on an unsuspecting world, that upsets people.

If recent trends hold, when human cloning is done it will not start with some egocentric millionaire who wants to have himself cloned in a secret laboratory on a remote island. It will almost certainly first be done in laboratories and clinics that specialize in human fertility and reproduction.

Indeed, research that lays the groundwork for cloning humans is already taking place. Many of the researchers who are doing this work either don't want to talk about it or just don't call it cloning. "Cloning," one of them said, "is a politically dirty word."

At one of the congressional hearings held in the wake of the announcement of Dolly, Dr. Harold Varmus said that it could take just one infertile couple, arguing that cloning provides their only chance to bear a child, to turn public opinion around.

Though human reproduction is supposed to be one ethically untouchable area, in reality most Americans have enthusiastically accepted massive scientific intervention. When techniques like artificial insemination, in vitro fertilization, surrogate motherhood, and fertility drugs were first announced the reaction ranged from caution to disgust. Yet when the first "test tube baby," a baby who was the product of in vitro fertilization was born, she was hailed as the "miracle baby" and the doctors who developed the process were heroes. To date some 30,000 babies have been born in the United States as the result of in vitro fertilization.

In November 1997, seven babies were born to a mother who had been taking fertility drugs. This was an event that was entirely "man-made" and arguably every bit as unnatural as cloning. But this too became a "miracle" covered in loving detail by everything from the supermarket tabloids to respected newsmagazines. Amid the chorus of praise for the "miracle mom" and beaming doctors who delivered the babies, the ethical and practical issues of having seven babies at one time were barely touched on.

In February 1998 a healthy baby was born from an embryo that had been frozen seven years earlier. It was another "miracle" birth.

Could the first cloned human child be greeted as a "miracle" rather than a monstrosity?

If the first human clone were produced from an adult cell and appeared as a photocopy of its "parent," the reaction would certainly be one of revulsion. But at the edges of reproductive technology the moral, ethical, and legal issues get very fuzzy.

For example, Dr. Mark Sauer, an infertility expert at the University of Southern California, says that he would like to use cloning in the treatment of some of his patients who had been unable to bear children. What he would do is take a human embryo, at the stage when it is two or three days old and has only about eight cells, and use the cells to grow identical embryos where there was only one.

He would then implant some of the woman's embryos in her uterus immediately and freeze others for future attempts at pregnancy. The woman might wind up with identical twins, triplets, or more over a period of years. The alternative might be no babies at all.

Sauer believes this procedure could be safer and more efficient than pumping the same woman full of powerful and potentially dangerous fertility drugs—a procedure that is not only accepted but applauded in American society today. Some researchers have said that work in this area is almost certainly going on right now, perhaps in several different laboratories.

Is creating the identical twin of an embryo that was never born really cloning? Sure it is. But in practice it wouldn't necessarily be called cloning. Is it morally acceptable to produce a human clone from an embryo and morally unacceptable to produce a clone from an adult cell? Again, the moral, legal, and ethical issues can become extremely fuzzy.

Critics of human cloning are quick to point to the failure rate. In the experiment that produced Dolly, Ian Wilmut started with 277 eggs and wound up with only a single sheep. But only thirteen of the eggs developed into embryos and twelve of the thirteen miscarried, a far better success rate than was achieved in the early days of the now-accepted practice of in vitro fertilization.

One of the scariest images to come out of the current cloning debate was that of people having themselves cloned and then using the clones to "harvest" organs needed to be transplanted into them when their own organs have failed. Today there is a critical shortage of organs for such surgery; many people in need of a transplant have died for lack of a suitable donor organ. There have been charges that physicians have oc-

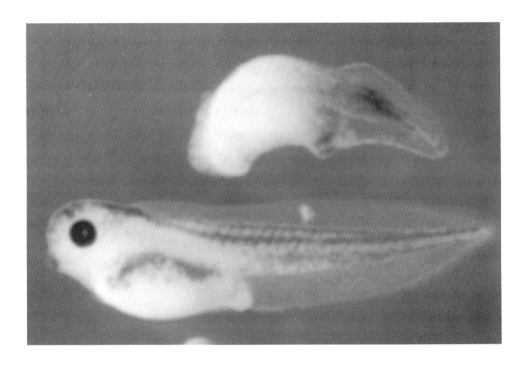

The embryo of a normal tadpole is shown below a cloned headless embryo. The uproar inspired by this photograph was probably fostered by a London newspaper article which reported that the technique was developed to see if organ and tissue farming was possible.

casionally been "harvesting" organs from people who are not really dead yet, or that the Chinese government has been "harvesting" organs from executed prisoners and selling them to rich people in need of an organ transplant.

In October 1997 a group of British scientists announced that they had been able to produce headless frog (actually tadpole) clones. It was feared that this research would ultimately lead to the production of headless human embryos to grow organs and tissues for transplants.

One newspaper columnist, Joy Thompson, envisioned a horror film titled *Night of the Organ-Harvesting Headless Humans*. The column concludes, "When it comes to human beings, cloning, genetic engineering, and organ harvesting are unconscionable, the stuff of horror movies. It should not be allowed."[5]

*Time* magazine columnist Charles Krauthammer envisioned a world in which headless people are cloned and stocked for spare body parts. He said this was a reason why all human cloning should be banned.

But what if a single organ could be cloned? This is not as farfetched as it may sound.

Most scientists believe that the most likely organ to be cloned first is bone marrow. Bone marrow is what is called a liquid organ. The cells do not have to arrange themselves in a specific pattern. Bone marrow makes the red blood cells that carry oxygen, the white blood cells that are the basis of the immune system, and the platelets that cause the blood to clot.

The process of cloning bone marrow, or any organ, is to start as if cloning an embryo. Then add chemicals that would direct the cloned cells, which possess the potential to become any part of the body, to become bone marrow cells.

Bone marrow transplants are critical in the treatment of many diseases, particularly leukemia. Many leukemia patients have died painfully for lack of bone marrow from a compatible donor. What if a patient could grow his or her own bone marrow that would be a perfect genetic match that would not be rejected, and could be used whenever needed? Is research into such treatments "unconscionable"? Should it be banned? Is it all a mad scientist's dream out of a grade B horror film?

While many would argue that any kind of research that involves human cloning at any level is the "slippery slope" that inevitably leads to the real horrors, are Americans really willing to deny a childless couple their only real chance to have a baby, or a person dying of leukemia a second chance at life? Probably not.

But where are the boundaries? Should there be any boundaries?

In the argument over cloning a lot of commentators have dug out a quotation from physicist Robert Oppenheimer, the scientist who headed the Manhattan Project, which developed the first atomic bomb:

"When you see something that is technically sweet you go ahead and do it, and you argue about what you do about it only after you have had your technical success."[6]

Dr. Steen Willadsen, who pioneered many cloning techniques, has echoed Oppenheimer's view a half century later, "It is not for me, as a person who invents techniques, to say how we should use them."

This book began with the statement that the idea of cloning seems to possess as much explosive potential at the end of the century as the idea of the atomic bomb had in the middle of the century.

Now you see why.

# CHAPTER 8

# THE FUTURE IS HERE

IS HERE

THE FUTURE

As the new millennium began, the debate over cloning became fiercer and weirder. Back in 1978, when the possibility of human cloning appeared to be remote and wild speculation, a furor was ignited by the publication of the book *In His Image: The Cloning of a Man*. It was a hoax.

In 2002 the furor was revived by a strange cult called the Raelians. But this time it was no hoax.

To call the Raelians strange is neither exaggeration nor insult. They are strange, by practically anybody's definition but their own. The cult was started by a French-born former racecar driver known only as Rael.

According to Rael, in 1973 he met up with space aliens whose flying saucer had landed on a volcano in southern France. Among his other adventures, Rael had an encounter with some very sexy female robots that had been created by the aliens. As is usual in such tales, the aliens gave their new human friend previously secret knowledge. This knowledge was that the human race had been created in a laboratory by other space aliens who had mastered genetic manipulation and bioengineeering. Cloning quickly became central to the Raelian doctrine.

For an article in *The New York Times Magazine*, writer Margaret Talbot describes a visit to the group's spiritual headquarters, UFOland in rural Quebec, and a meeting with the secretive, bearded prophet himself, wearing his "characteristic samurai-style topknot, white pants, wide-shouldered white tunic and gold medallion."[1] According to Rael the topknot and his beard serve as antenna, by which he receives messages from space.

He told the interviewer of his vision of cloning adults and then "uploading" the adult memory into the new body.

Even in the post-Dolly era this is still the stuff of science fiction, and the Raelians could easily be brushed aside as just another fringe UFO cult—except for Clonaid. Founded in 1997 by Rael, Clonaid bills itself on its Web site as the world's first human cloning company. The Raelians' ultimate goal is personal immortality through cloning. Their first step is to clone a human baby, which they say they are trying to do right now.

The Raelians were contacted by a well-to-do American couple, the parents of a ten-month-old baby boy who died in the hospital after a minor operation. They had some of the boy's cells frozen, and became obsessed with cloning the dead child. They found the Raelians through the Internet and agreed to finance an effort to clone the boy. The parents have since withdrawn support, but the Raelians are not without their own resources. Worldwide, they have somewhere between 25,000 and 50,000 members, and millions of dollars. They claim that they already have a small team of physicians and scientists working on the cloning project somewhere in the United States, though they won't say exactly who or where. Most significantly, they say they have at least fifty young female group members who are eager to act as egg donors and surrogate mothers. This core of healthy and committed volunteers would be absolutely essential to the success of any human cloning project.

Virtually every reputable biologist and geneticist strongly and loudly disapproves of the Raelians and what they are trying to do. They also don't think the cult has much of a chance of succeeding in cloning a human. But they can't rule out success entirely, not anymore. Advances in cloning have been coming faster than anyone had predicted just a few years ago and some of the advances are coming from unusual places. Dolly had been cloned in an obscure farm animal research facility in Scotland. And that had surprised just about every leading biologist and geneticist in the world.

Matters came to a head in August 2001 when Brigitte Boisselier, a French chemist and the scientific director of the Raelians' Clonaid company, was one of three members of a panel of human cloning advocates to appear at a meeting of the prestigious

National Academy of Scientists in Washington, D.C., to answer questions from some of their skeptical—and sometimes downright hostile—colleagues.

The other two members of the panel were Professor Severino Antinori, a flamboyant and highly controversial Italian human fertility specialist, and his associate, Panayuiotis Zavos, a professor of reproductive physiology at the University of Kentucky. Even before his appearance in Washington, Professor Antinori (or "Dr. Miracle," as he is sometimes called) had achieved a considerable measure of fame, though notoriety might be a better word, in Italy and throughout Europe.

Professor Antinori operates three very successful fertility clinics in Italy. He is known for stunts such as the "millennium baby," where he implanted embryos in fourteen women so that the babies would be delivered seconds after midnight on January 1, 2000. But what made Antinori famous was *le mamme-nonne*, roughly translated as "the granny-mommies," women who had gone through menopause but were able to bear children through assisted-reproduction techniques. In 1994, Antinori helped a sixty-two-year-old Italian farmer's wife deliver a child. She became the oldest woman at the time to give birth. This project was controversial in 1994, and has remained so. The Italian medical association has threatened Antinori with the loss of his right to practice medicine in Italy, and Pope John Paul II has denounced his work. Antinori's bid to locate a cloning lab in Israel was decisively rejected by the Israeli parliament. Indeed, he has been greeted with hostility by so many countries that he has spoken of establishing his cloning lab aboard a ship in international waters.

Opponents have compared Professor Antinori to Dr. Frankenstein, a comparison he rejects. He has other models. "I am like Galileo or Alexander Fleming. When they discovered things, they were accused of being controversial. In the whole of scientific history, people have been accused of playing God when it's not true."[2]

Clearly, the flamboyant Italian doctor is not easily discouraged. At the National Academy of Sciences meeting in August 2001 he announced that he and his associate, Professor Zavos, were ready to begin human cloning attempts within two months.

At the time of this writing there is no evidence that human cloning for the purpose of reproduction is actually seriously being attempted either by Professors Antinori and Zavos, by the Raelians' Clonaid, or by anyone else. There are rumors, of course, but no solid evidence. Yet as Gregory Stock, the director of the Program on Medicine, Technology and Society at UCLA's School of Medicine pointed out, "what they're doing is of symbolic significance. If they don't succeed, someone else will in five years."[3]

The appearance of the three human cloning advocates at the National Academy of Sciences created a virtual media frenzy, with reporters and photographers shoving one another to get a close-up or a quote. One bioethics professor complained "It's like Barnum and Bailey circus." Scientific meetings are generally more sedate affairs with little outside press coverage.

From the left are Severino Antinori, the Director of International Associated Research Institute, Panayuiotis Michale Zavos, Director of The Andrology Institute, and Brigitte Boisselier, Director of the Raelians' Clonaid company. The three appeared together on a panel in support of cloning at the National Academy of Science in August 2001.

Certainly the appearance of the three human cloning advocates was not popular with many other cloning researchers. Dr. Ian Wilmut, who had created a similar frenzy back in 1997 when he and his associates cloned Dolly the sheep, had earlier refused even to appear on the same program with Professor Antinori because he did not wish to give Antinori credibility.

The National Academy of Science appearance did not, however, create, or even reignite the cloning debate. It merely turned up the heat a bit on a pot that was already in full boil. Most European governments had voted to ban human reproductive cloning research completely. There was no such blanket ban in the United States, but such a ban had been enacted in several states, and the U.S. Congress was already debating the subject as well. The terrorist attacks of September 11, 2001, disrupted all normal congressional business, and for a time pushed the cloning debate off the front page. However, it is all but certain that an overall ban on human reproductive cloning of some sort will be enacted by Congress at some point, and will be enthusiastically signed by President George W. Bush, who has frequently expressed his dislike, even revulsion, for the idea.

There are numerous religious, moral, and ethical arguments against human reproductive cloning. Many of these have been discussed in earlier chapters, and these arguments have not changed in the new millennium. But there are also practical and scientific considerations. And here the ground may have begun to shift a bit.

The most powerful practical argument against human cloning is that it is very hard to do. In animal experiments the vast majority of clones—as high as 90 percent—do not survive to full term. Among those who survive there is a high percentage of severe abnormalities, and many of these abnormalities are not apparent before birth.

In January, 2002, it was announced that Dolly, the famous cloned sheep, had developed arthritis. This condition in not uncommon in sheep, but Dolly appears to have developed it at a very young age. Are her cloned cells aging prematurely? No one knows, and according to Ian Wilmut, the scientist who cloned Dolly, it is impossible to know if the cloning process is to blame.

One discouraged cloning researcher says that the attempt fails so often that success is "a biological accident."[4] Scientists often do not report negative results, while the tiny number of successes get a great deal of attention. That gives the public the impression that cloning research is moving along much more quickly than it really is.

No one really knows why cloning fails as often as it does. The cloning process itself, taking the nucleus from one cell and placing it into an egg from which genetic material has been removed, is difficult and delicate. Some researchers seem to develop a feel for the careful manipulation of microscopic cells; others do not. The embryos first begin to develop in the laboratory, under a wide variety of subtly different conditions that are not really understood. Cloning is, in many ways, still more of an art than an exact science.

Take the experience of Dr. Randall Preather of the University of Missouri. For years his laboratory tried to clone pigs. But the experiments always failed. Then quite suddenly they began to work, but Dr. Preather had no idea what changes in laboratory procedure made the difference. Other scientists who have engaged in cloning experiments have had similar experiences—they don't know what caused the problems, and don't know what solved them, or what caused a once successful program of experiments to suddenly begin to fail.

Some species seem to be easier to clone than others. A higher percentage of mouse clones develop than cattle clones. Again, nobody seems to know why.

Some cloning critics insist that cloning never really works properly. "I don't think there is a single normal clone in existence," Rudolph Jaenisch, a professor of biology at the Massachusetts Institute of Technology, told a congressional hearing early in 2001. That view, however, has been strongly challenged by scientists at a company called Advanced Cell Technology in Worcester, Massachusetts.

The Advanced Cell Technology scientists say that they have created twenty-four cloned cows that are completely normal. "We ran every medical and scientific test that was available," Dr. Robert P. Lanza, medical and scientific vice president of the company, insisted. "Everything is perfectly normal."[5]

Another cloning pioneer, Dr. Steen Willadsen, who cloned more than a hundred cows from embryo and fetal cells back in the 1980s, said that while he did not do detailed tests of the clones, they all seemed healthy enough.

According to Dr. Willadsen, "At this point it does not seem reasonable to maintain, as some have said, that all cloned animals are abnormal."

But Dr. Jaenisch counters by saying, "You have to define what normal is. Subtle changes are very had to detect." Variations might not be of great concern to cattle, but they would be of great concern in a human clone.

In mid-August 2001, a group of scientists from Duke University added fuel to the human cloning debate when they published a study indicating that humans may possess a genetic characteristic that makes us less vulnerable to fetal abnormalities than mice, sheep, cows, or other animals commonly used in cloning experiments. The highly technical and complex study was published in a journal called *Human Molecular Genetics*, not a widely read magazine. Usually such a study would have attracted the attention of only a tiny handful of specialists. But in the supercharged atmosphere surrounding anything that has to do with cloning, the Duke University work became big and highly controversial news. Dr. Randy Jirtle, author of the study, insisted that he was not advocating human reproductive cloning: "We are just presenting information."

Some proponents of human reproductive cloning insist that human cloning would have a far higher degree of success because doctors who work with human fertility already have decades of experience with some of the very same procedures that would be necessary in human cloning. These are, in fact, the procedures that have been used, with great success, in Professor Antinori's clinics.

The couple that got in touch with the Raelians were trying to replace a dead child. That goal makes a lot of people very uncomfortable.

Replacing a dead pet seems not only benign, but downright warm and fuzzy. There are currently companies that collect DNA from pets and store it indefinitely, though cloning is not yet available. Clonaid has a division dedicated to pet cloning. Gene banks typically send a DNA collection kit, which a veterinarian uses to take a small skin sample. The tissue is grown in a culture and then frozen in liquid nitrogen, ready for thawing and cloning in years to come. How many pet DNA samples are currently frozen for future cloning is unknown, but it is more than a few. So far, no dog or cat has ever been successfully cloned, though many attempts have been made. Why it is more difficult to clone a dog than a sheep, no one knows.

Down at Texas A&M University there is the "Missyplicity" project. The anonymous but very wealthy owners of a dog called Missy are spending several million dollars on research to have their pet cloned.[6]

Texas A&M, an agricultural university, has been criticized and ridiculed for the project. But the school has done a lot of experimenting with animal cloning other than the Missyplicity project. They are working on cloning cows that will produce more milk or will be resistant to certain diseases, and cloned pigs that can be used as human organ donors.

A&M scientists have cloned a litter of pigs, which may help provide important insight into cloning. Cloned cattle and sheep produce only one offspring at a time. But a litter of pigs gives scientists a chance to study several clones at once.

In the first cloned pig litter one of the piglets was much larger and more aggressive than the others. And there was a small, timid "runt" of the litter. "We're seeing some pretty drastic differences in the body weight and behavior," Jorge Piedrahita, head of the pig-cloning project, told reporter Kris Axtman of *The Christian Science Monitor*. "What that tells us is that small differences in environment can cause large differences in personality."[7]

The university is also engaged in projects to clone endangered species such as the Atwater prairie chicken and desert bighorn sheep. Cloning can help save these rare animals from extinction.

"You could repopulate the world with [an endangered species] in a matter of a couple of years," says H. Richard Adams, dean of A&M's College of Veterinary Medicine. "Cloning is not a trivial pursuit."

And then there is Second Chance, a 1,000-pound (454-kilogram) Brahma bull born in 1998. Second Chance is the clone of Chance, a pet bull, who at the age of twenty-one was the oldest animal ever cloned.

Chance was a sort of celebrity who appeared regularly at rodeos and county fairs and was in several movies.

Chance's owners are delighted with the results. Ralph and Sandra Fisher say it is just as if their old friend is still alive. "This is not a son or a twin brother," says Mrs. Fisher. "It's him."

Second Chance not only looks like the original but apparently acts like him, too. For example,

Chance's favorite spot was in the front yard, just outside the kitchen window.

"The day we brought Second Chance home, he lay down in the same exact spot. And the first time he saw Ralph, he loped across the pasture toward him, licking his face and his boots," Sandra Fisher says. "I'm a little hesitant to say he has his memory, but he has the same instincts. Let me put it like this: Given the same problem, Chance and Second Chance would figure it out in the same way."[8]

Now, is that warm and fuzzy? Or is it kind of creepy? I guess it depends on your point of view.

# CHAPTER 9

# THERAPEUTIC CLONING

CLONING

THERAPEUTIC

Most public attention has been focused on the area called reproductive cloning—reproducing an entire creature, be it frog, sheep, dog, or human being. As the twenty-first century unfolds, it is far more likely that what has been called therapeutic cloning—cloning used to cure disease—is going to have a more immediate impact on all of our lives. Your chances of getting a cloned liver are greater than your chances of seeing a cloned you.

In Chapter 7 we briefly discussed the possibility of using cloning to provide spare parts for humans. It was a prospect that provoked outrage and shudders of horror among opponents of cloning and the general public. But research in this area has progressed much more quickly than research in reproductive cloning. And the issue has become a lot more complicated.

Much of the argument has centered on what are called "stem cells." Most cells in the human body possess a full genetic code—that is, they have all the genetic information necessary to make another human being. But as we develop from infancy to adulthood cells become specialized, or differentiated. DNA related to other functions shuts down, or somehow loses the "memory" of how to become another part of the human body. The cells that make up the heart will do only that; they will not become brain cells or liver cells, even though they have the DNA to do so.

Some work has been done to attempt to reverse the process of differentiation in developed cells. But it's easier to use undifferentiated cells—stem cells. Stem cells appear only during the very earliest stages of embryonic development.

Stem-cell research holds the promise of tremendous scientific and medical advances. The research can help science understand how tissues regenerate. This knowledge can lead to effective treatments for Parkinson's and Alzheimer's diseases. It may also hold the key to procedures that could restore tendons, ligaments, cartilage, and bone, and therefore heal crippling diseases and injuries. Farther down the road is the possibility of growing whole new organs. It is hard to overestimate the medical benefits that might flow from stem-cell research. It's also hard to overestimate the amount of money that can be made from developing these treatments.

Getting stem cells for biological research does not necessarily involve cloning. There are several ways they can be obtained, and the easiest and richest

# Stem Cell Cultivation

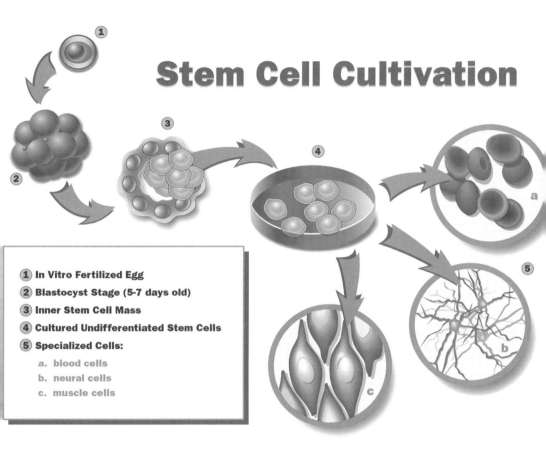

1. In Vitro Fertilized Egg
2. Blastocyst Stage (5-7 days old)
3. Inner Stem Cell Mass
4. Cultured Undifferentiated Stem Cells
5. Specialized Cells:
   a. blood cells
   b. neural cells
   c. muscle cells

This illustration shows the very early stage at which stem cells can be collected. Five to seven days after a egg is fertilized, stem cells can be harvested. For people who believe that life begins when the egg is fertilized, stem cell research is not justified.

source seems to be fertility clinics. Human embryos are created in the laboratory as the first step of the *in vitro* fertilization process. But there are usually many more embryos created than are actually used. These surplus embryos are either kept frozen in storage or destroyed.

However, using such embryos for research, even if they look like little more than a splotch in a petri dish, runs smack up against the deeply held moral and religious convictions of a great many Americans. In their view, the embryo must be treated as a person from the moment of conception. It's the basic point of contention in the long-running and emotional debate over abortion.

Not all abortion opponents also oppose all stem-cell research. But there is enough opposition for this scientific, medical, moral, and religious issue to also become a hot political issue. The political side of the issue is not a ban on all stem-cell research in America, but only on research that is funded by the federal government. This is where the issue of money plays such a large role. The sort of basic research needed for rapid advances in the field is extremely difficult and expensive. Private companies, which must show a quick profit, are not likely to fund this kind of research because a company that spends hundreds of millions of dollars on research that will not pay off for years, and very possibly not pay off at all, is not likely stay in business for long. So if the federal government cuts off funds for basic stem-cell research, progress will be dramatically slowed.

In August 2001, President George Bush announced that federal funding for stem-cell research could continue, but on a limited basis. Federal funds could only be used for research involving already established stem-cell "lines," that is, cells derived from embryonic tissue that had already been used in biological research. He described his decision as one of the most difficult that he had ever made in his life.

Neither side in the debate was really satisfied. Those who believed that any kind of research with embryonic cells was immoral, and that even limited stem-cell research was a "slippery slope," were disappointed that a president who had staunchly proclaimed his anti-abortion stance would not draw a clear moral line.

On the other side, those who favored more research complained that the limitations would severely hamper progress in an area that held the prospect of alleviating so much human suffering. They also complained that the presidential order had grossly overestimated the amount of stem-cell material that would be available for use in federally funded research.

The debate was sure to continue, but like so many other political debates in America, this one was also temporarily buried in the ruins of the World Trade Center on September 11, 2001.

By late November the debate was back.[1] Now the issue of cloning was at the center. The small but aggressive biotechnology company Advanced Cell Technology of Worcester, Massachusetts, announced, with much fanfare, that their scientists had taken the first steps toward cloning human embryos. The ultimate goal, according to the company, was not to produce fully developed human clones, but embryonic stem cells for further research in therapeutic cloning. Indeed, the DNA used in this study came from a paralyzed doctor. One of the great hopes of therapeutic cloning is that tissue produced from a patient's own DNA will not be rejected when transplanted back into the patient's body.

In reality, what Advanced Cell Technology had actually done was far less dramatic and significant than it had first appeared. Most of the cloning attempts failed, and the small number that did succeed stopped developing after just a few hours and died. The experiments were a long way even from producing the embryonic stem cells, and could easily be classed as failures.

The techniques the company's scientists had employed were not new, either. They had long been used in animal cloning.

But the announcement itself stirred up the cloning debate once again. In the U.S. Congress, opponents of cloning renewed their efforts to pass a ban on all human cloning. At a news conference President Bush said: "The use of embryos to clone is wrong. . . . We should not as a society grow life to destroy it."

The company announcement also drew criticism from many who favor stem-cell research and the promise of therapeutic cloning. They felt that they had been making some quiet progress in convincing lawmakers and others that they were not mad scientists on a Frankenstein-like quest. Now this elaborately publicized and overhyped announcement will, in the view of University of Pennsylvania bioethicist Professor Glenn McGee, "make a sober debate about stem-cell research impossible—and even endanger the future of such research in this country."[2]

Still, *New York Times* medical reporter Gina Kolata, who has chronicled the progress of cloning research since Dolly the sheep, wrote: ". . . if there is a future in human cloning, either for reproduction purposes or to create cell lines for use in treating diseases people may one day say it started in Worcester."[3]

And beyond that lies the promise, or the threat, depending on your point of view, of genetic engineering, which makes even the dreams of the Raelians seem modest.

The cloning controversy that began with Dolly will be with us for a very long time.

# NOTES

NOTES

## CHAPTER 1

1. Jessica Mathews, "Post Clone Consciousness," *The Washington Post* (March 3, 1997), p. A19.
2. Robert G. McKinnell, *Cloning: A Biologist Reports* (Minneapolis: University of Minnesota Press, 1979), p. 12.
3. Aldous Huxley, *Brave New World* (New York: Harper, 1946), p. 16.

## CHAPTER 2

1. Michael Specter and Gina Kolata, "After Decades and Many Missteps, How Cloning Succeeded," *The New York Times* (March 3, 1997), p. A1.
2. Gina Kolata, "Workaday World of Stock Breeding Clones Blockbuster," *The New York Times* (February 25, 1997), p. C8.
3. Rick Weiss, "Lost in the Search for a Wolf are Benefits in Sheep's Cloning," *The Washington Post* (March 3, 1997), p. A3.
4. Gina Kolata, "Workaday . . ." p. C9.

## CHAPTER 3

1. Nancy Duff, "Clone With Caution," *The Washington Post* (March 2, 1997), p. C1.
2. Susan Cohen, "A House Divided," *The Washington Post Magazine* (October 12, 1997), p. 16.
3. David Lebedoff, "The Clone Ranger: Double Jeopardy," *St. Paul Magazine* (July, 1997), p. 14.
4. Katharine Q. Seelye, "Clinton Bars Federal Money For Efforts to Clone Humans," *The New York Times* (March 5, 1997), p. A14.
5. Gustav Niebuhr, "Suddenly Religious Ethicists Face a Quandary on Cloning," *The New York Times* (March 1, 1997), p. A10.

6. Jane Gross, "Thinking Twice About Cloning," *The New York Times* (February 27, 1997), p. B1.
7. John Garvey, "The Mystery Remains," *Commonweal* (March 28, 1997), p. 7.
8. Leon R. Kass, "The Wisdom of Repugnance," *The New Republic* (June 2, 1997), p. 17.
9. Jane Gross, "Thinking . . ." p. B1.
10. Leon R. Kass, "The Wisdom . . ." p. 17.
11. Richard Dawkins, "Thinking Clearly About Clones," *Free Inquiry* (Summer, 1997), pp. 13–14.
12. Ronald Bailey, "The Twin Paradox," *Reason,* (May 1997), p. 52.

## CHAPTER 4

1. Willard Gaylin, "The Frankenstein Myth Becomes a Reality: We Have the Awful Knowledge to Make Exact Copies of Human Beings," *The New York Times Magazine* (March 5, 1972), p. 21.
2. William Safire, "Clonalities," *The New York Times* (February 27, 1997), p. A23.

## CHAPTER 5

1. Charles Pellegrino, "Resurrecting Dinosaurs," *Omni* (Fall, 1995), p. 68.
2. Charles Pellegrino, "Resurrecting . . ." p. 68.
3. Rob DeSalle and David Lindley, *The Science of Jurassic Park and The Lost World* (New York, Basic Books, 1997), p. 27.
4. Rob DeSalle, *Science of Jurassic Park,* p. 43.
5. "No DNA From Dinosaurs?" *Discover* (September, 1996), p. 18.
6. Jay Maeder, "Bring 'em Back Alive," *U.S. News and World Report* (October 13, 1997), p. 12.

## CHAPTER 6

1. Philip Siekevitz, Letter to the Editor, *Science* (October 15, 1976), p. 6.
2. Freeman Dyson, Letter to the Editor, *Science* (July 2, 1976), p. 6.
3. Gina Kolata, *Clone: The Road to Dolly and the Path Ahead* (New York: William Morrow, 1998), p. 113.

4. Charles McCabe, "On Playing God," *The San Francisco Chronicle* (April 14, 1997).
5. Gina Kolata, "Lab Yields Lamb With Human Gene," *The New York Times* (July 25, 1997), p. A18.

## CHAPTER 7

1. Rick Weiss, "Animals in U.S. and Europe Now Pregnant With Clones," *The Washington Post* (June 28, 1997), p. Al.
2. Rick Weiss and John Schwartz, "Monkey Clones Raise Human Issues," *The Washington Post* (March 2, 1997), p. A4.
3. Lawrence H. Tribe, "Second Thoughts on Cloning," *The New York Times* (December 5, 1997), p. A31.
4. George Johnson, "Ethical Fears Aside, Science Plunges Ahead," *The New York Times* (News of the Week in Review, December 7, 1997), p. 6.
5. Joy Thompson, "Scientists Should Think Twice About What They're Proposing," *The Long Beach Press Telegram* (October 29, 1997), p. B8.
6. George Johnson, "Ethical Fears . . ." p. 6.

## CHAPTER 8

1. Margaret Talbot, "The Cloning Mission: A Desire to Duplicate," *The New York Times Magazine* (February 4, 2001), p. 40.
2. Glenda Cooper, "The Double Vision of 'Dr. Miracle'; Human Cloning Proponent Faces Scientists," *The Washington Post* (August 8, 2001), p. C1.
3. Margaret Talbot, p. 40.
4. Gina Kolata, "In Cloning, Failure Far Exceeds Success," *The New York Times* (December 4, 2001), p. F1.
5. Gina Kolata, "24 Cow Clones, All Normal Are Reported by Scientists," *The New York Times* (November 23, 2001), p. A33.
6. Kris Axtman, "Quietly, Animal Cloning Speeds Onward," *The Christian Science Monitor* (October 14, 2001), p. 3.
7. Kris Axtman, p. 3.
8. Kris Axtman, p. 3.

CHAPTER 9

1.  Gina Kolata with Andrew Pollack, "A Breakthrough in Cloning? Perhaps and Perhaps Not Yet," *The New York Times* (November 27, 2001), p. A1.
2.  Glen McGee, "A Cloud Over Cloning," *The Philadelphia Inquirer* (December 2, 2001), p. D5.
3.  Gina Kolata with Andrew Pollack, p. A1.

# BIBLIOGRAPHY

Cherfas, Jeremy. *Man Made Life.* New York: Pantheon, 1982.

Crichton, Michael. *Jurassic Park.* New York: Knopf, 1990.

DeSalle, Rob and David Lindley. *The Science of Jurassic Park and the Lost World.* New York: Basic Books, 1997.

Facklam, Margery and Howard. *From Cell to Clone.* New York: Harcourt Brace Jovanovich, 1979.

Huxley, Aldous. *Brave New World.* New York: Harper, 1946.

Hyde, Margaret O. *Cloning and the New Genetics.* Hillside, NJ: Enslow, 1984.

Judson, H.F. *The Eighth Day of Creation.* Simon and Schuster: New York, 1979.

Kolata, Gina. *Clone: The Road to Dolly and the Path Ahead.* New York: Morrow, 1998.

McKinnell, Robert G. *Cloning: A Biologist Reports.* Minneapolis: University of Minnesota Press, 1979.

Rorvik, David. *In His Image: The Cloning of a Man.* Philadelphia: Lippincott, 1978.

Shelley, Mary. *The Annotated Frankenstein.* New York: Clarkson N. Potter, 1977.

Silver, Lee M. *Remaking Eden: Cloning and Beyond in a Brave New World.* New York: Avon, 1997.

Watson, James D. *The Double Helix.* New York: Athenaeum, 1968.

———, and John Tooze. *The DNA Story: A Documentary History of Gene Cloning.* San Francisco: W.H. Freeman, 1981.

# INDEX